S0-BXV-809

APOSTLE ISLANDS
N A T I O N A L   L A K E S H O R E

Kate Crowley and Mike Link

Additional Photography by
Don Albrecht   Paul Chalfant   Daniel J. Cox
Sean Heckman   John and Ann Mahan   J. Steinke

Wheaton Public Library
225 N. Cross
Wheaton, Illinois 60187

VOYAGEUR PRESS

To Ken and to Daisy,
who stood beside us
on our happiest day.

Copyright © 1988 by Mike Link and Kate Crowley.

Photos Copyright © 1988 by Don Albrecht: pages 6, 13, 22, 41, 58, 70.
Photos Copyright © 1988 by Paul Chalfant: pages 12, 37, 42
Photos Copyright © 1988 by Daniel J. Cox: this page, pages 28, 35, 36, 45, 48, 50, 51, 53, 66
Photos Copyright © 1988 by Kate Crowley: pages 17, 18, 28, 64, 65, 69, 85, 89, 90, 96
Photo Copyright © 1988 by Sean Heckman: page 73
Photos Copyright © 1988 by Mike Link: pages 24, 25, 67, 78, 79
Photos Copyright © 1988 by John and Ann Mahan: front cover, back cover, title page, pages 4, 8, 9, 10, 14, 21, 26, 27, 28, 32, 37, 46, 56, 57, 60, 62, 63, 73, 74, 75, 76, 80, 83, 86
Photo Copyright © 1988 by J. Steinke: page 85

All rights reserved. No part of this work may be reproduced or used in any form by any means—graphic, electronic, or mechanical, including photocopying, recording, taping, or information storage and retrieval system—without written permission of the publisher.

Published by Voyageur Press, Inc.
123 North Second Street
Stillwater, MN 55082 U.S.A.

ISBN 0-89658-084-9

88 89 90 91 92 5 4 3 2 1

Printed in Singapore by Singapore National Printers Ltd
through Four Colour Imports, Ltd., Louisville K Y

CONTENTS

INTRODUCTION

Writing about the Apostle Islands is a difficult exercise, only because of the limits of time and space. Kate and I have had so many wonderful experiences here that we must fight the compulsion to share everything.

My own wanderings in the islands began on Outer Island over two decades ago. I was left off by a powerboat and spent a solo weekend experiencing a quiet bay.

My first sailing trip was out of Cornucopia, when the captain lost control and we were knocked down near the caves of Squaw Bay. It would have made sense for that to be my last sail, but it seemed to stimulate rather than scare me.

Since then, I have returned often, to bicycle Madeline with students, to camp with another class on the Sioux River beach, to skinny-dip in Big Bay on a quiet September evening and then to sleep under the stars, as cold and quiet took over. But it is sailing that has called me back, that has deepened my love of the islands.

Kate I were married on the *Izmir*, the 42-foot ketch that we sail for Northwoods Audubon Center. It was tied to the visitor dock at the Madeline Island marina and festooned in red and blue pennants. The sky was bright and sunny, a wind had carried us and our guests on a series of tacks between Madeline and Long Island, and my spirits were inflated by the breeze and the beauty.

Our honeymoon trip culminated on July 4, when we sat anchored in a bay as the sunset colors flowed across the water from the hills behind Bayfield. We grilled steaks, and as we toasted with champagne, the fireworks lifted from the barge in the Bayfield harbor. Their bursts were doubled in the reflection of the water, but the sound was lost in the distance.

Now every trip is an extension of that event. Every ski or sail is a continuation of our honeymoon. We have grown to appreciate the dedication of people like Jerry and Mary Phillips, who work to enhance the Bayfield economy while trying to keep its growth within the beauty of its surroundings. They know that natural beauty is the area's best asset. We also respect the Park Service and their efforts to maintain the islands. We may disagree on some decisions, but we do agree on the purpose of the National Lakeshore designation—the preservation of the island ecosystems.

We hope that our book will share some of these values with you. We also hope that we might entice you to find a quiet place and discover the Apostles for yourself.

Boat graveyard in Bayfield. (J. and A. Mahan)

(D. Albrecht)

6

IMAGES

Patches of green on a mat of blue; a roaring surf, curling white rollers on red clay banks; red apples in rich green foliage; grey fog and the black silhouette of shoreline cedars; blinking and rotating lights of yellow, white, and red cutting through a blanket of blackness; white clouds suspended in an arch of brilliant blues; multicolored sails, white-flecked waters, and bending trees. The Apostles are an archipelago, a cluster of islands, an unlimited collection of experiences, and a montage of sensory images.

The scents of the islands: Sweet spice wafts from the basswood blooms, and an invisible force field of vibrations surrounds the tree as honeybees buzz in a feeding frenzy. The only fragrance that can match the basswood's is the pungent spicyness of the trailing arbutus — small white bell-like flowers that lie in the forest litter. To capture their scent you must lie on the ground, where the smell blends with the earthiness of the spring humus. In the domestic setting, the orchard rivals these natural potpourris. The trees are a blizzard of white, and the breeze is an invisible river of essence.

The tastes: First think of the astringent taste of cherries, the wild kind that pucker the mouth. The wintergreen plant has a waxy coating to protect its volatile spirits, but when you chew it, you can almost feel a candy mint resting on your tongue. The beach pea is crisp, and its taste recalls that summer walk down the garden path when you drop rich, green peas into your mouth.

The sights: You envision the dramatic: hot-pink lady slippers, green carpets of club moss, wands of goldenrod waving in the wind. But can you remember the small cones of the hemlock beneath your feet, like marbles on the path?

Then touch: the web of the spider across the morning path, that tacky feeling on the face as you move like an insect into its invisible net. Feel the sharp contrast between the burning sediments of the high-noon beach and the cold water that contracts the expanded blood vessels of your feet, quickly and almost painfully. There is the shudder of relief in the skin as an ice cream cone melts on your tongue in the August heat at Bayfield. Water running down the neck of a rainslicker becomes magnified in size and coolness as it bends the small hairs on your neck and spine.

The hairs on your body are like the tactile organs on insects, feeling motion, relaying messages about external factors. Standing on deck on a hot day with the wind blowing lightly is sensuous — you can feel the heat leaving the body.

There is the smoothness of the water-polished driftwood, a smoothness that can be stroked, and there is the soothing smoothness of wave-tumbled volcanic rocks along Outer Island's eroded clay banks. These rocks are worry stones, the kind that you can rub absentmindedly while you think. The sandstone looks smooth, but when you run your hand over its surface, the grains of an ancient delta catch on the ridges of your finger, tugging your mind to ancient streams in lifeless valleys.

There is a contrast between sun and shadow. Is there an intermediate temperature? You sense the heat and the coolness, but is there a transition or a wall between the two?

Your feet respond to the solid resistance of the rock, the treadmill of moving sand particles, and the spongy texture of forest litter.

The twig of the spruce is armored with sharp needles, while the fir and the hemlock have blunt leaves. The sphagnum in the wet areas not only holds water, it holds all the other plants, and the trampoline sensation that comes from walking on it is emphasized by the bowing of trees far in the distance.

And there is sound: the wind in the pines sets up a roar that exceeds the actual strength of the air movement. The needles bend along the twig, funneling the air like airfoils in a jet engine.

The water that surges beneath the worn rock ledges slaps and bangs. Sounds carry up the cracks and echo in the hollows. You hear spirits, and the islands seem alive.

Warblers move quickly through the tree tops, trailing small songs that seem to come from the leaves. Gull calls on the water tell of old ships, and fishermen. Gulls are the sound of the sea, although there are no such things as "seagulls." Halyards clang against the mast. To the sailor, it means someone didn't tighten them and there will be a racket to contend with all night. To those who walk the docks and dream, it is a sound that entices, that calls you to sail into the horizon.

The more sensations we notice, the more satisfying the experience. It is a more detailed "painting." Merely looking is like eating with a plugged nose—it means sacrificing the depth of the experience. The islands bring together many landscapes and many images. We sprinkle the present with the past, land with sea, mid-continent with coastline, reality with dreams. The Apostles are a place to slow down, absorb, and take home contentment.

Planks and timbers from an old shipwreck in Julian Bay—Stockton Island. (J. and A. Mahan)

Wintergreen and reindeer lichen. (J. and A. Mahan)

(J. and A. Mahan)

HOW MANY ISLANDS?

"Welcome to the Apostle Islands."

"They sure seem pretty, are there twelve of them?"

Another introduction to the confusing pattern of the Apostle Islands is about to begin, with a navigational map of the islands spread before us.

"No, there are twenty-two islands, although one of them is not an island (Long Island), but rather a sand-spit peninsula that occasionally gets separated from the mainland by major storms. It's been a long time since one of those storms has been around."

This explanation doesn't always end the confusion, but by using the chart we can navigate through the islands' history.

★   ★   ★

Twelve is a common expectation because of the twelve Apostles, but there is no clearcut explanation of this name. Some historians claim that the Jesuit missionaries were confused as they entered the islands and perceived only twelve. That would have merit if they only passed by; but the missionaries set up a school here, and math was included. The more convincing explanation considers the beauty of the islands and the Jesuits' desire to honor the Apostles by naming a beautiful place for them.

Another possibility is that when Father Pierre Xavier de Charlevoix came to the Great Lakes in 1721 as an agent of France, he didn't actually visit Lake Superior but relied on the voyageurs, who referred to the islands as the Twelve Apostles. We can guess that many of these men could not count. Jonathan Carver and Lewis Cass later gave Charlevoix credit for naming the group.

Another theory is that a group of freshwater pirates operated in the islands and waylaid the unsuspecting fur trader and entrepreneur. The pirates were said to have called themselves "The Apostles." They may have existed, but the name Apostles was associated with the islands before the pirates were.

At this point, we have to mix history and geology to see how great an error "the Twelve Apostles" really is. We can eliminate Long Island from our discussion quickly. Not only is it not an island, it lacks the bedrock and the clay of both islands and mainlands. It is a barrier beach, a very large barrier that is formed by longshore currents. The Long Island barrier beach was usually not included in early island reports, but Radisson did report making a portage there. John Johnson, a 1790 resident, wrote that he saw twenty-six islands; and Henry Schoolcraft, Indian agent and Mississippi River and Lake Superior explorer, gave the islands twenty-eight or twenty-nine names. He tried to change the island group's name to the Federation Islands. He then proceeded to give each island the name of a state or territory. This may have eliminated the confusion between the number of islands and the number of Apostles, but it certainly was not aesthetic.

Twenty-six, or twenty-eight or twenty-nine? Then where are the missing islands?

Islands with Indian, missionary, explorer, mapmaker, and voyageur names have vanished like ghost ships in the fog of history, but their tracks are still on our modern charts. Blue water on the white chart marks shallow places, places of history and danger. Each of the shoals may represent an island, or an extension of an island, that was ravaged by storm and now exists for fish spawning and shipwrecks.

A quick survey of the chart shows the following shoals: Bear, York, Sand, Eagle, Oak, Devils, Outer, and Gull. All of these are named for the nearest islands, but only Outer appears as an extension of its namesake. These could have been the missing seven islands from Schoolcraft's account, except that there is another factor that we have not looked at: The movement within the lake may also combine islands.

On Stockton Island, Julian Bay is the plum; it is the most picturesque beach in the islands. Beyond the beach is an open water area and then a large campground. The campground is an old beachline, a curving arc that surrounds Presque Isle Bay and forms the island's most popular anchorage.

This is an area of ridges, of old pines and dunes. It is a succession of beaches from various stages of lake development and it is a bridge (geologists refer to it as a *tombolo*, which means "bridge" in Italian) that joined a large island to a small island, now known as Presque Isle Point.

When Lieutenant Bayfield mapped Lake Superior in the 1820s, he identified two islands where York Island now stands. York's beach is also a tombolo, as is the beach where the fishermen's cabins sit on Rocky, and maybe the beach on Cat. If we include Presque Isle, this means at least four more islands were in the Apostles.

Thirteen more islands—thirty-four in all (if we ignore Long)—may have existed here. But were there ever thirty-four at once? Gull probably separated from Michigan, and South Twin may have once included what is now the east arm of Rocky. Given more time, Rocky may join Otter, and Gull may disappear completely.

Confused? No more than the person who tries to trace each island's name. They were named by the Ojibwa, and some of those names still persist. But in addition to the Indian and Schoolcraft names, there must have been many other enterprising cartographers around, because Madeline Island has had at least twenty names. Its history of names includes the translation of Ojibwa, the Island of the Golden-Breasted Wood-

pecker; the French Isle Detour, La Pointe, St. Esprit (which was the mission name), Michel, La Ronde (a French commandant), and Montreal (because many of its inhabitants were educated there); a variety of English names; and Schoolcraft's Federation Islands name—Virginia.

Most of the remaining Indian names are in a translated version. The exception is Chequamegon, which has also been spelled with *J* and with *S* as the first letter and with numerous combinations of letters for the rest of the word. Its meaning has also been obscured, so no single translation remains, just lots of explanations.

The confusion is perhaps best illustrated in an 1848 book by Charles Lanhan that must have enlightened many readers. The author made a "pilgrimage" around the lake by canoe and wrote of his exploits. Of the Apostles he says, "The group consists of three islands, and they stud the water most charmingly." (It can only be hoped that not all of Mr. Lanhan's information had this degree of accuracy.) His literary adventure was probably confused by maps that called Madeline "Middle Island", a reference to the island's position as a midway point between Sault Sainte Marie and the western end of Superior.

In 1893, the Ashland paper noted that it would be possible to connect the islands by a series of bridges (the Florida Keys of the North?), which might have helped us count them, but would have killed their spirit and beauty at the same time.

A rocky shelf juts out on the east side of Devils Island. (P. Chalfant)

(D. Albrecht)

On Madeline Island, there is an old cemetery, where many of the original settlers and Indians are buried. Madeline was the Christian name given to the granddaughter of the Indian chief White Crane. (J. and A. Mahan)

THE ANISHINABE

The story of the creation of land has many variations, each people adapting the story to their particular location. In the case of the Apostle Islands, the story involves Winabojo. In Ojibwa legend, he was both a supernatural being and a mortal who was sent to the world to teach the Anishinabe, to help the weak, and to heal the sick.

Winabojo was involved in a conflict between the wolf and the sea lion. The wolf disappeared and the sea lion was killed, and the sky poured down water to wash away the tragedy. Winabojo was left clinging to the top branches of one white pine that escaped the flooding.

The land and water were in chaos, and Winabojo needed to set things right. He called first to Nigig (the otter) and ordered it to dive to the bottom of the water and bring up sand so that Winabojo could create new land. The otter was gone for many minutes; the water was too deep, and its lifeless body came floating to the surface. Winabojo breathed new life into it and sent it on its way. This same sequence was repeated with Amik (the beaver) and Mang (the loon), and still there was no land.

Finally Wajashk (the muskrat) was summoned and sent into the depths. Its body also floated up lifeless after many long minutes beneath the surface. As Winabojo took the muskrat's form in his hands to breathe back life, he discovered a few grains of sand between its claws.

Winabojo took these wet grains and blew on them until they were dry. He then cast these upon the water, where they became the seeds of an island. From the island more sand was taken and scattered until it grew to sufficient size so Winabojo could plant life and begin anew. This was La Pointe, on Madeline Island.

Life was good, but it was not enough. The unbroken expanse of water needed more land, so Winabojo cast sand from his island into the open water and created the islands that we call the Apostles.

★ ★ ★

The American Indians followed the melting of the glacier; they walked the ancient shorelines and they hunted the muskox and mammoth. The Indians were on the shore of an iceberg-studded lake; they were there as the tundra turned to forest and as the lake levels changed.

The story of Winabojo has its counterpart in geology, in the mammals that swam into the lake from the connection of the Saint Lawrence seaway, a time when all the Great Lakes were one. The Indians were here to see walrus and sea lion, and they were here to see the lakes separate and the levels drop below sea level, and then to watch the lake reestablish itself without the marine mammals.

On ancient beachlines are archaeological sites that give evidence of humans' presence as part of the ecology that established itself after the ice age. The pieces of pottery, the nut and charcoal fragments, and the few animal bones that have been found are insignificant in and of themselves; but together they are a reminder of the continuity of the American Indian. Their campsites are located where we would choose to put our campsites today, a testimony to the unbroken flow of human spirit and needs.

These were not primitive people; they were people living within their means, within the available resources. They are referred to as Paleo Indians, the Old Copper Culture, the Woodland Cultures, and then the tribal peoples—the Sioux and the Chippewa—but these are not their true names. In fact, *Indian* is a term that was given to the Native people by Europeans who were so confused that they thought they were on another continent.

The Anishinabe, as they call themselves, moved from salt coast to freshwater coast, from the Apostles to the Sault and back, caught between the pressures of the Iroquois in the East and the Dakota (Sioux) in the West. The Anishinabe were part of the Three Fires Confederacy, the largest Indian alliance, with the Cree in Canada and the Potawatomi on Lake Michigan. The odyssey of this Ojibwa nation is told in the following story.

Manitou communicated to the Indian through the sky, the colors of sunrise and sunset being the color of the Indian and the sacred Megis Shell. This shell, a saltwater shell, brought the Indian prosperity, but it was an illusive shell, which seemed to drift from the people periodically and leave them in famine and suffering.

The disappearance of the Megis Shell caused the chiefs to send out scouts for its sign. The first great move was from the Saint Lawrence to Sault Sainte Marie; the second was to Madeline Island, which represented the center of the earth, the beginning place. The Indians settled here and prospered, but famine followed, and the Ojibwa moved around Lake Superior until they eventually returned to the place where they would stay.

Madeline Island was the site of a *Medawegaun*, a ceremonial house in which the fire of unity was maintained. It was a place of peace, a place where the Midewiwin rites were performed. Later it would be the place of the missionary, of the competing Catholic and Protestant churches. The sacred island would mix sacred symbols.

In the sweat lodge, the stones were arranged like the Pleiades, known as the Sweating Stones (*madodisson*) in Ojibwa astronomy. *Jibekana* (the Milky Way) was the path of souls. The North Star (*Giwe danang*) had the same name and performed the same function for all the ethnic groups, but the Indian sky also contained *Noadji Manguet* ("the men who walk behind the loon," just behind the North Star and the bear's head), the bear's cross, and the three traveling kings, who have no counterpart on our sky charts.

When cultures meet, they seldom blend, and they never melt—they adjust, they clash, and the strongest dominates. The Dakota and the Ojibwa clashed, and wars enhanced by trade rifles reduced both nations. The hidden enemy, disease, cut into the populations; overconsumption through trapping and trading affected the Anishinabe independence; and ultimately the trader demanded that the Indians foresake their ancestral religion and adopt the European brand.

Fewer and fewer Indians lived their traditional life in the wilds. They were removed to reservations by the treaty of 1854; their free world was shrinking. The Red Cliff Reservation was made for the Catholic Indians, the Bad River was for the Protestants; there was no reservation for the *Mides* (the Indian religion).

Peace between Indians was accomplished with a flourish, similar to the signing of treaties between the USA and Russia. Buffalo Bill came to Ashland in 1896 to oversee a treaty that would give his Wild West Show new publicity. The "Chippewa Indians" were represented by the four Wisconsin reservations, and the Dakota representatives were all employees of the Wild West Show. The media were important in those days too, and Colonel William F. Cody ordered an extra six hundred copies of the local newspaper for his own use.

★ ★ ★

I stood with Acorn on the dock at Stockton Island and he pointed to the clearing across the bay. "I would go over to my grandparents' campsite just past the park's campsite number 20, and place a feather where the old fire pit once was. Then I would just sit and meditate."

Francis Gordon, also known as Acorn, is a park employee, a maintenance man of Stockton Island, and a brother of Bill Gordon, who is the interpreter on Manitou Island and the unofficial greeter of Stockton campers. He is the essence of the island. Misnamed a maintenance man, Acorn is an attraction. His personality is bubbly, his smile is infectious, and his relationship with the island exceeds the information that any other green-clad park employee can impart.

"Dad was a World War I veteran, a French Canadian/Indian. On my father's side, Jesse Davis married a Gordon from Fort William. She told me, 'You are lucky, you can fall in love and choose now. In my day a canoe would come over and the chief would trade gifts for his son's wife.' Maybe that's how she got married. She also told me that to have a child a woman went out behind the bushes by herself, and then she would bring the child back in to the others.

"My maternal grandfather, Bressette, had blue eyes and reddish blonde hair. It was the Bressettes that I would stay with on Stockton."

When he was ten or eleven years old, he would sit in the famous tree trunk (near site number 15) that is along the camp path, the tree with a sideways **S**, and contemplate the pleasures of the island. Here were deer, fish, and berries. Here they could play and learn.

"They would sell their berries at the co-op in Bayfield, or trade them for groceries. We would hunt deer a lot; there were a lot more of them at that time. When a deer was taken it was shared with all the families, six or seven of them, then what was left was tied to a string and submerged in the bay. There was a stick on one end that would float and the cold water would preserve the meat.

"I would play in the water with a stick that had a rubber-band-powered propeller.

"There was a camp at Trout Point, too. It was infested with rabbits, so Dad made a bow out of cedar with a big knob in it. He drew an arrow, and when he let go it just dropped at his feet. The rabbits stood and watched it.

"Father took me out in the woods and taught me a lot. One time he asked me what I would do if I was lost. I told him that I would backtrack—follow my own tracks. He said, 'That's good, you have the instinct of an Indian.' I really got mad when he said this; I thought he said that I had the stink of an Indian.

"One time a porcupine was crawling by and I said, 'I want that porcupine.' Dad told me I couldn't have him because the porcupine belonged in the woods. I was mad, I could be a bad boy, and I sat down and refused to go. I had this fine shotgun and I shot off the branch of the tree it was in. The porky walked into a hollow log and I tied a rope around its feet. I pulled him

16

and his quills stuck in the log." Acorn then pulled both the porcupine and the log out of the woods. "When we got out of the woods my dad asked, 'What now?' I couldn't think of anything so I let it go."

Acorn's dad was very independent and would not stay on the reservation. Off the reservation, the taxes were high, and Acorn's mother gardened to help meet their needs.

Near retirement now, Acorn has worked as a Madeline Island greenskeeper, played in country western bands, cut wood, worked on an ore boat, fished for Boutin, been a machinist, and worked for the Park Service in maintenance. In the early 1950s he achieved some fame from a *Field and Stream* article that told the story of "The Big Buck of Basswood Island"—

describing a hunting trip that he helped guide.

He is the father of fifteen and grandfather to thirty. He is a religious man, a musical man, and a man of the islands. When he was young his dad saw him playing a broom as if it were a guitar, so he got Acorn a real one. For three years nothing happened, then "all of a sudden I got the sound." Now the guitar is an extension of Acorn's feelings and sensitivity.

Perhaps the light in the sky is still communicating with the Red Cliff Indians. Acorn's lyrics are his meditations.

> "It sure feels good to wake up in the morn on Raspberry Island.
> I thank God for the Sunset glow, it makes me think of things I miss, of my life so free."

Park employee Francis "Acorn" Gordon shares his knowledge of Stockton Island, where as a child he camped with his family (K. Crowley)

17

VOYAGEURS

All seascapes are boatscapes, all places where people and water come together are places where boats are a dominant theme in history. Today we see the sailboats, excursion boats, and ferries, and they are joined by paddlers in canoes and seakayaks. The popularity of big-water paddling seems like a new phenomenon — the small boat in the large waves paddling toward blue horizons seems out of place — until we think of the rich history of these islands. The Indians did not cruise in yachts, nor did the explorer and voyageur move around in motor launches. Their craft were powered by paddles that opened the lake to development and began the inevitable flow of history.

Today the boats are changed; the seakayaks are closer to the Inuits' boats than to the voyageurs', but they are still an intimate association between paddler and place. The canoes are made of materials that were not in existence in the voyageurs' time, and their designs are computer generated for stability, tracking, and the least wind resistance. But it is still human muscle that makes the boat move. It is skill that controls the boat's position on the waves, that guides it toward the next island, that avoids the catastrophe of being cast on the rocks where water and wind are more powerful than any manmade material. Distant beaches, solitude, self-reliance, and personal fortitude are still the ingredients of an island paddle.

The first non-Indian to paddle here may have been Brulé, or it could have been Radisson and Groseilliers. Whoever it was followed a lakeshore that was already known, that had inhabitants from headwaters to outlet; the momentous significance of their effort was beyond their ability to comprehend. When they reached Kitchigumi (later Grand Lac, and then Lake Superior), they had extended the hand of history to the very center of the continent.

When they came here in small boats, their fates could have been changed by one storm, and history would never have proceeded to what we know today. Radisson and Groseilliers disembarked on a wilderness shore and found streams abundant in beaver, forests rich in timber and game, waters filled with fish, and Indians with whom they could establish commerce.

They had struck the trader's gold, and boatloads of furs moved from the Apostle region to Montreal. The explorer/traders thought that they had a lifetime's wealth, as well as fame, but government intervened. France and the fur industry declared that they had been in violation of the law, that the furs were taken illegally, without a license and without the mandatory Jesuit to accompany the party into new lands. The furs were taken, the men were thrown into prison, and a sequence of events was set in motion that would establish the Hudson Bay Company and a competition between the British, French, Canadian, and American nations.

History is often based on the pratfalls and accidents of time, the seemingly inconsequential events and individuals. This one stirred up the French and Indian Wars, and three different flags would fly over Madeline Island.

The fur trade was destined to return, even if the original participants would not, and Madeline Island was the strategic point for the post that would oversee it. This time the trader had as a partner a Jesuit — first, in 1661, it was Father Menard, who disappeared on a trip inland during his first tour of duty, and then it was Claude Jean Allouez.

The voyageur was a blend of nationalities — French, Canadian, and Indian were predominate, but there were black voyageurs, English, American, Scottish, and an assortment of others. They were the boatmen, not the entrepreneurs. They blazed trails and portages, but were unaware of economies and politics. They paddled from dawn until dusk, fueling their bodies with beans and pemmican, fish and game. They knew the Indian as another canoeist, and yet they were tied to the whims of Montreal, London and Paris.

The first of the French commanders in the Apostles was Pierre Le Sueur, who later would explore and establish forts on the Minnesota River. The remainder of

The dock at the Raspberry Island lighthouse attracts boaters of all persuasions. (K. Crowley)

19

the commanders were insignificant names in commerce, but noteworthy was Madame La Ronde, who took over from her husband for five years. Women in the fur trade were unheard of, and even her story was only a note in an old historical book that I read.

There were many different posts, missions, and buildings at La Pointe over the years. After the French and Indian Wars it fell under the British flag; and Alexander Henry, one of the legends of the fur trade, received rights to this area. He was fortunate to have as his partner Jean Baptiste Cadotte, who ran the island post with greater efficiency than the site had ever seen.

Cadotte settled here, planted roots and crops, and made himself a part of the land. His son, Michel, married Traveling Woman, granddaughter of the Indian chief White Crane, had her baptized Madeline, and fathered a family that still lives in the area.

Other traders left stories, if not legacies. John Johnston, who was Scots-Irish, came to the islands, named the area Netougan, and ran his voyageurs with a strict hand—until the free spirits among the employees listened to the suggestions of the French voyageurs and staged a revolt. His company took his canoe, his food, and some of his trade goods, and left him to become the Robinson Crusoe of the Apostles.

Johnson had a 17-year-old companion, whose name is lost in history. This "Friday" and the "Crusoe" Johnson cut wood and prepared for winter, but it was the aid of the Indians in the area that really allowed them to survive. The result of this alliance was Johnson's marriage to the chief's daughter, and subsequently their daughter, who would become Madeline.

Missionaries continued to be a major influence on life in the islands. Allouez had his mission burned by the Ottawa Indians before he left for an around-the-lake tour. He was replaced by Father Marquette, who won notoriety as an explorer as well as a missionary. All the missionaries, the Jesuits and the Protestants, had to venture over the waters, but none was more of a canoeist than Father Baraga.

Father Baraga was from Austria, a man of moderate wealth and good education. In 1831, he went to the mission fields and spent five years with the Ottawa Indians in Michigan. He next moved to Lake Superior, where he spent thirty years, nine of them at La Pointe. He was physically strong, and enjoyed the exertion of long canoe trips. On one trip, he was crossing the lake to the North Shore and encountered a storm part way across. To any boater, a storm on Lake Superior is frightening; to a birchbark-canoer, it must be terrifying. The party weathered the storm and landed near the "Cross River" in Minnesota, where the missionary built a wooden cross before delivering a sermon to the Indians and then recrossing the lake.

The missionaries recorded Indian history; the school "civilized" the island; the voyageur and the Indian fished, hunted, raised crops, raised children, and made maple syrup in idyllic surroundings. The Northwest Company fought the Hudson Bay company, Sieur Du Luth built a fort (Fond du Lac) on the Saint Louis River, Grand Portage became the rendezvous place, the Americans surplanted the British flag on Madeline and caused the British to develop Fort William near present-day Thunder Bay. Companies with names like XY and American controlled the island trade, and the fur industry vanished. But La Pointe did not. It is the oldest town in Wisconsin, with the longest continual history, and its future looks bright.

La Pointe controlled the western half of the lake; it was the marketplace, the central exchange. Then the tributaries of Fish Creek, White River, Marengo River, Bad River, Montreal River, and Brule River ran out of beaver. Other places became more important for exchanging furs for pay goods. The post should have died, but it didn't, because then as now it was surrounded by abundance.

Beaver brought wealth, but voyageurs needed to eat; and when the region did not produce pelts, it did provide fish and agricultural produce. The voyageur history was one of diversification, and as a result, their paddling songs echoed in the rocks longer than anywhere else on their trade routes. Today, paddlers join these songs, perhaps sensing the ancient cadences as they listen to the echoes in the sea caves and hollows in the rock. The paddler today is immersed in the pleasure of the passage, just as the voyageur of long ago. It is not the promise of money that makes a paddle fit the grip of a hand, it is not threats that cause the canoe to journey toward the mirages, nor is it a quest for immortality that drives the boat through wind and wave. It is a journey of spiritual direction, it is a merger of "self" into the complex of "place," and it is an ancient rhythm of basic earthly ecology.

Clothing and equipment used by the voyageurs are displayed in the Madeline Island Historic Museum—the old fort in La Pointe. (J. and A. Mahan)

21

THE ROCK CUTTERS

The woods have ventured forward with tentative roots to reclaim the cracks and crevasses in the sandstone. Fern and moss form ribbons that mark the separation between layers and mining history. In the pit, a watery carpet is green along the edges with duckweed, but reflects the straight walls and sharp corners. Time is the tool of nature, reclamation is a natural process, and soon the forest will reside where humans do not keep it out.

The rock is reddish, and each layer of stone marks a period in the history of our earth. It is a Precambrian stone, a part of the earth that dates back to a period long before there were roots, or any other living matter. It was a time when weather and rock and water shared the earth equally, and the planet shaped and reshaped itself in forms we can only imagine.

That is the charm of geology—it is an exercise in imagination, tempered by science. Science fiction writers can never move beyond the reality of geology—volcanics, gravity, atmosphere, physics, and atomic structures. They only play along the edge of the fantastic. The geologist is the most transcendental of all scientists; their magic is the ability to ignore watches and calendars, to float with atoms in a timelessness, to realize that all atoms on earth have been in existence since the beginning of the planet, and to understand that the atoms that make up each one of us may have been rocks at one time too.

Geologists follow the tracks of rocks and landforms and perform the ultimate detective work. They see the layers in the quarry as time and energy held in limbo. They know that the rock masses are static only because we have such short life spans. They are the authors of science nonfiction, and their worlds are as exciting as those of Heinlein and Asimov.

When they touch this rock, the grains that are locked in place take them to a time when the great Penokean Mountains loomed on the southern horizon, below Chequamegon Bay, beyond the city limits of Ashland. They can picture grand peaks with clouds floating beneath their crests and snowy shawls around their shoulders. These were as grand as the Alps, but there were no cameras to record their glory.

They rose and then fell without ceremony. Their earthquakes are recorded in ancient rock beds and their molten interior is the backbone of the North Country Trail. The exterior of these mountains crumbled beneath rain storms. Rocks were priced loose by the expansion of water into ice, and the wedges plummeted off cliffs and rolled down avalanche shoots, breaking into mineral bits and crushing the rocks they collided with. The rocks worked downward from the peaks to the valleys as each new process etched the mountain. Finally, small grains tumbled into the streams that filled the valleys, and small streams flowed to larger, and on and on to the ocean itself.

From the Penokean Mountains, the sand grains of these great mountains traveled to a massive basin that would eventually be part of a great river system that sprawled to the east in old faults and bedrock structures. Here, at the edge of the valley, the river discharged much of its load. It must have fanned out, unrestricted along the shorelines. Like the great streams of Alaska, the waters separated and rejoined in great braids, with thin layers of sediment beneath the moving water and bars and beaches of thick sand where the current was blocked and the streams separated. The seasonal fluctuation of flow caused the streams to cease, and the sediments that were being carried were deposited to fill the channel, putting thick beds above thin.

As you go along Devils Island today, the beds, both thick and thin, are obvious, as is a slight dip to the south. Perhaps the sediment that came off the mountains was so thick near the source that the layers compressed the earth. The dip is slight, but on Devils, the thin-layered rock near water's edge is where the caves can be found. In the quarries, the thick-bedded materials are sought. The difference in strength is visible to us in our boats.

An old abandoned sandstone quarry on Basswood Island gradually disappears as the forest takes over. (D. Albrecht)

There was a period of time when the Apostles were a relatively flat terrain and the rivers began to carve the area instead of building it. The new streams were not carrying the load of disintegrating mountains, they were merely moving the rain waters to the lowest elevation. The river that dominated our Superior basin, and now the plain of sandstone, represented the high country. The streams found pathways in cracks, and deep valleys were carved, moving the landscape from plateau to mesas.

As the valleys deepened, side streams left the new high lands and dissected into buttes, much like the process that is visible in the Theodore Roosevelt National Memorial Park in North Dakota. This was the shape of this land when the glaciers came.

The massive sheets of ice rumbled over the landscape and icy fingers slid up each valley, widening and sculpting the bottoms, rearranging the landscape once more. The evidence of their coming can be found in the quarries too. Above the quarry walls are boulders of material other than sandstone, left by the melting ice.

All of that energy is locked in the rocks, all of that history is exposed in the quarries. Run your hands in the grooves of the quarry operation. Feel the smooth channels, find the marks of the chisels and sit upon the steps that were carved. It takes you to a much more recent history, a time of humans and their focused energies, applying great pressures that were far more concentrated than the glaciers'.

From the 1860s to the turn of the century, men were using steam energy to remove the sandstone from the islands. There were two quarries on Basswood Island, the first one started by Captain Sweet and a Milwaukee investors group. The metal ring in the rocks on Basswood is still there, a mute witness to the old operation.

On the mainland there were quarries near Bayfield—one is easy to observe on Highway 13, and others are near Cornucopia and Port Wing.

As many as seventy-five men worked the quarries on Stockton, and four separate brownstone companies ran the quarries on Basswood, Hermit, and Stockton islands. They were excavating for building stones, for

The sandspit on Outer Island is the largest in the Apostle Islands. (M. Link)

a structural rock that had been tempered for over one billion years, that would be used to construct row-houses, libraries, courthouses, and other large edifices. In those days before steel girders, architects were limited by the constraints of nature.

Massive blocks were taken from the quarry to the docks, where derricks placed them on barges. The barges moved the big slabs to the mainland, and there they were loaded onto big ships. Little by little, the foundation of the islands and the peninsula was moved to Duluth, Milwaukee, Chicago, and Detroit, to become part of the foundation of the cities.

The old excavations are muted by time, but new excavations continue as the wind generates power and waves rework the shoreline, leaving isolated rocks on the east side of Basswood, Hermit, and Stockton. They are aesthetically more varied than the human quarries, but they are only isolated remnants of island cliffs that once extended much farther than they do now — part of the evidence that the landscape, even the bedrock, is far from static.

Overleaf:
The northeastern shoreline of Devil's Island is pockmarked by sea caves that have been carved out of the sandstone through centuries of wave action. (J. and A. Mahan)

25

Rain-washed apples. (D. Cox)

Blueberries. (J. and A. Mahan)

SUMMER SWEETS

In the Apostles, you could alter the calendar and exchange the words *June, July, August,* and *September* for *Strawberry, Raspberry, Blueberry,* and *Apple.* These are the real treasures of the islands. And it's not necessary to expend great sums of money to uncover the wealth of sweet booty. You need only time, patience, and a strong back.

Long before the European emigrants arrived in the islands, people were reaping the bountiful harvests of fruit. And before the native Americans discovered these natural treats, the wildlife knew about them. Today, people and wildlife compete for the taste of summer sweets that grow wild on the islands.

Before the fruits even begin to form, the beautiful, fragrant blossoms appear. Strawberries, raspberries, and apples are all from the rose family. In spring, with the reawakening of the land, the air is filled with the perfume of flowers opening to the warmth. Apples bloom high above ground, where their scent is easily carried on a spring breeze, while the flowers of the strawberries and raspberries are much closer to the ground and require almost direct contact for perception of their perfume. The blueberries are in the heath family; their flowers have a subtle sweet smell that demands that you kneel and press your face close to the blossoms.

Two common attributes of the wild fruits are their small size and an intensified flavor not found in domesticated varieties. It requires a great amount of effort to pick a bucketful of these cherished berries. When people discovered that fruits could grow so well on the islands and the Bayfield peninsula, they decided to try to improve on Mother Nature by planting hybridized, domesticated species of strawberries, raspberries, and apples. These are typically larger than their wild counterparts. They are more easily harvested and can be grown in large enough quantities to be financially rewarding.

Everywhere you go, you will see signs advertising the current fruit harvest. Some eating establishments in Bayfield almost fill their menus with some variation of the fruit—blended, baked, sautéed, pureed, and a la mode.

STRAWBERRIES

People have differing opinions, of course, but many will tell you that the strawberry (genus *Fragaria*) is the most delectable of all the berries. Growing close to the ground, strawberries flourish in open meadows and near forest edges. They need sunlight to ripen fully, but cannot tolerate too much dryness. Look closely and you will see thin horizontal runners that extend from the base of the plant in search of new and suitable soil. The leaves and flowers grow on separate hairy, slender stalks. The flowers are white and five-petaled, with notched outer edges. Underneath the petals are five-pointed leaflike sepals and five bracts (which are modified leaves).

You know a strawberry is ripe when it comes off easily in your hand. Berries picked too soon make the mouth pucker, while those that are ripe release a combined odor and flavor that makes me hum with satisfaction.

So often, food that tastes delicious is said to be "bad" for us. No so the strawberry. They not only taste wonderful, they're good for you, too. Rich in vitamin C, they also contain iron, potassium, sulphur, calcium, sodium, silicon, and related malic and citric acids. Native Americans knew of their medicinal value and used them to treat colds, while the early colonists made tea from strawberry leaves for the prevention of scurvy.

In the islands, our competition for the harvest of the wild strawberry comes from squirrels, rabbits, white-tailed deer, and lots of birds, especially the robin. As with many other fruits, the birds and animals don't seem to mind eating the unripened berries, so by the time they are ripe enough for our tastes, the crop has already been well picked over.

The harvest of wild strawberries is truly a labor of love, for they seldom grow bigger than one-half inch long. It would take many hours of back-bending picking to fill a bucket with these tasty morsels, but even a handful is enough to spoil one permanently for any other kind.

RASPBERRIES

According to wild-foods expert Bradford Angier, raspberries are the most valuable wild fruit on this continent, in terms both of money and of importance as a wildlife food. He says there are anywhere from fifty to four hundred species of raspberries/blackberries (genus *Rubus*) in the United States alone, depending on whether the botanist classifying them is a "lumper" or a "splitter."

The cultivated varieties are generally more expensive than strawberries, possibly because their size does not increase appreciably with domestication and they are difficult to protect from animals. Harvesting raspberries in the wild is not an easy task. In this case, it is not the bending of the back that causes pain, but the pricking from the thorns that line the stems of the plants.

Raspberries, sometimes called brambles, grow shrublike, sometimes as high as six feet, and the bristly red or green stems arch over one another in moist, sunny thickets. The stems (canes) have a life span of only two years. The first year, the root system sends up the long, unbranched canes. These produce leaves but no flowers. The following year, the canes produce side branches, which produce the flowers and later the berries. After that, the canes die back; the following spring, the two-year cycle is repeated. The black raspberry (often called blackcaps) is able to root from the tip of the arched branch.

The flowers on the branches are white and five-petaled, and drop soon after blooming. If you look closely at the center of a flower that has dropped its petals, you will see a miniature green raspberry. The berries are composed of many small sections, each with a small projecting hair, which is actually the former pistil of the flower. The hairs remain on the berry as it grows and changes from green to red; and when the berry is picked, the hairs give a fuzzy feeling.

Raspberries are an aggregation of drupes (juicy pulp-filled ovals containing one hard seed). You notice this much more easily after the fruit has been cooked and made into a jam. The seeds resist crunching, planting themselves in the spaces between your teeth. If you look at the plant after removing a berry, you will see a soft spongy cone at the tip of the stem. This is the original flower's receptacle, where many ovaries clustered together to form the drupes.

A ripe raspberry easily separates from the stem; in fact, once it's ripe it won't wait for you to pick it—it will fall to the ground. You can be sure that the wildlife on the islands will be ready to catch any fallen and falling raspberries.

The shrubs produce such a thick and impenetrable mass that small animals and birds use them as a source of cover. Then, as the berries ripen, the creatures are right there to enjoy them. Somehow deer are able to eat the thorny stems as well as the leaves.

In July, you should begin to look for the ripe berries. They will provide you with a good dose of vitamin C—some have 2 and one-half to three times as much as an orange (though if left in the sun after being picked, they quickly lose their vitamin value). They make excellent wines and liqueurs. In researching raspberries, I came across an interesting recipe for a nonalcoholic beverage. It is made by soaking ripe raspberries in vinegar for a month, straining, sweetening to taste, and then diluting with iced water.

BLUEBERRIES

This fruit has not been cultivated in the area, but it can be found on many of the islands. Members of the heath family, blueberries require an acid soil and light shade. They depend on fire to control other plant competitors. Now that the Apostle Islands are a National Lakeshore, fires will be managed, to imitate natural wildfires.

Francis Gordon is a native American who grew up in Red Cliff, across from the islands. Talking to me on the dock at Stockton Island, he points across the water to an opening in the forest farther down the bay. That is where he and his family would go each summer to pick blueberries. Now he sees fewer and fewer berries each year.

The early Americans, who roamed in small hunting/gathering groups, used blueberries for food and dyes. The berries could be dried or charred and preserved for the winter months. And as anyone knows who has spent some time picking the little blue balls, they stain the skin. Alone, they make a blue-grey dye; mixed with nutgalls, they produce a rich brown dye or ink.

Blueberries grow in clumps and clusters of small woody shrubs. The branches zigzag and the bark is covered with numberous speckles, or "warts," but is free of thorns. Height varies from highbush to lowbush varieties, but in the islands, I have only seen the lowbush, which measures eight to fifteen inches above ground. The flowers are small, white, pinkish, or greenish, and bell-shaped. They grow together in clusters at the end of the branch. When the berries ripen, they have a star-shaped pattern on the end away from the stem. This resembles the opening on the flower.

Blueberries contain hundreds of seeds, but unlike with strawberries and raspberries, we don't even notice them, they're so small and easily chewed. The same birds and mammals that feast on the other fruits will be found eating blueberries. To the earlier lists, you can add black bears, which are especially fond of blueberries. It is easy to identify the large dark piles left behind by a foraging bear.

When we take people sailing in later summer, we always try to provide them with time to pick blueberries on Stockton Island. Some bushes are found along the trail near the campground and others are found on the trail leading to the bog, but the best bushes are found on the sandy dunes above Julian Bay. The berries are small, and a person could spend an hour picking a pint's worth. Many of our passengers volunteer to share their pickings, especially when they learn that Mike is willing to cook them in the morning pancakes.

Cleaning the picked berries is also time-consuming. One source I read said that blueberries grow so thickly on the bushes that you can often spread a sheet on the ground and merely shake the branches and have your harvest. I have yet to find any blueberry bushes that behave in this way. Normally, it is a slow process, picking one or more at a time, and as your patience wanes, more leaves and stems are added to the pail.

We usually put the picked berries in a colander and run water over them, then put them in a pan of water and attempt to float the debris to the surface. A pioneer method, which I have not tried, suggested pouring a few at a time onto a slanted, preferably new and fuzzy wool blanket stretched tightly a few feet below. The ripe berries roll into a large, wide container placed below the bottom edge of the blanket, while most of the harder, greener berries will bounce free. Leaves and other debris catch on the blanket, which can be brushed from time to time.

Visitors to the islands come back year after year for the chance to reap the harvest of the wild blueberries. We think it is important to understand the connection between fire and these fruits, for the future may require the periodic burning of some land if the blueberries are going to continue to satisfy our tastebuds. Park visitors, by their concern and comments, can affect the management of the fruits.

APPLES

Malus pumila — the "forbidden fruit." Of all the fruits in the Garden, God chose to put the apple off-limits. Could you see Eve holding out a blueberry or even a raspberry? No, an apple is a fruit you can really get a grip on. If it is polished just a bit, you can almost see your own image in the shining skin. Was Adam blinded by his own handsome face peering back at him? The first bite into an apple is never silent — if God hadn't been watching, there would still have been the telltale crunch as Adam sunk his teeth through the apple's tight skin and juicy hard pulp.

And so paradise was lost. But somehow, the apple came away from the episode with a much better reputation than did the snake. In fact, today we say "mom, home, and apple pie" all in the same breath of respect.

Domestic apple trees originated in Asia and southeastern Europe and were brought to this country by the early settlers. They hybridize easily, and today, by either accident or cultivation, there are more than three thousand varieties.

In the spring, apple trees are explosions of pink or white that bring joy and hope to the winter-weary resident of the northland. Branches are covered with the sweet-smelling blossoms, each with five perfect petals and five sepals. In the center is a cluster of yellow pollen-topped stamens and one pistil, which will develop into the apple.

On the Bayfield peninsula, apples have grown to be a major source of health, wealth, and happiness. In 1847, when the American Fur Company occupied the islands, there were already three apple orchards in existence. Hermit, Sand, and Basswood islands all had some plantings of apple orchard, but none could top the undertaking of the lighthouse keeper on Michigan Island. His name was Pendergast and he was an accomplished nurseryman. By 1870, he had planted twenty thousand fruit trees on the island.

For continuous and successful business, apples require great care and husbandry. The islanders came and went, and the orchards were eventually overgrown by the more assertive vegetation. Even so, it is still possible to find an apple tree here and there as you hike on the islands. The best ones are probably well hidden and known only by the deer, bear, and songbirds.

In Bayfield, the culmination of the summer season is the Apple Festival, held every October since 1950. A big sign hangs over the street, proclaiming "Bayfield — The Apple of the Isles." The day before the festival is one bustling with last-minute preparations. A stage is being built in front of the grocery store, concession stands are going up along the sidewalks. Many will hold apples, but there will be lots of arts and crafts for sale too. Parking areas are flagged off outside of town for shuttle service; the streets in town will be barricaded to traffic. Beer trucks rumble past, and people line up at the Indian fried bread booth, located near the gazebo.

The sun shines with early October brightness on a mountain ash that grows between the hardware store and another building. It mimics the apple trees with clusters of red-orange berries. A cold wind blows down Rittenhouse Avenue as the Trollers, the high school marching band, begin to assemble near the main pier. They are dressed in candy-apple-red blazers. This harvest fest glorifies the color red.

There are street entertainers, apple-peeling contests, pie-baking contests, decoration and costume contests. An Apple Queen is crowned, and the weekend is finalized with the Apple Festival parade on Sunday afternoon. And everywhere there are apples for sale, bags of Cortland and McIntosh — red and green and golden yellow. The sweet-tart taste of freshly picked and pressed apple cider is available by cup or jug. It is a celebration of the bounty of nature and the fruit of the garden.

A cricket has become a meal for this carnivorous pitcher plant that grows in the island's bogs. (J. and A. Mahan)

THE NATURE OF THE ISLANDS

Ever since Darwin made his historic journey to the Galápagos Islands, people have looked at islands in a different way. Island ecology provides a look at the evolution of species, as well as a laboratory for biological interactions. Islands represent isolation, the chance for varying groups of organisms to experiment with life without the full range of competition and predation to contend with. Islands like those in the Galápagos and the Hawaiian groups have a history that goes back to the early periods of life itself, and they are isolated by hundreds of miles from other land masses.

People have also been interested in the isolation of the Apostles, but these islands have a history that is only a few thousand years old and they are only a few miles apart. Consequently there is no Apostles Island finch or Outer Island tortoise. What is there is still interesting, however, because we want to know how it got there. The absence of some animals that live on the mainland is also a curiosity.

To get to an island, any organism, whether plant or animal, needs a means of movement. It can float across, as does a seed, or a small mammal on a raft of flood debris; it can fly, swim, or cross the ice; it can use the wind for transport (even small amphibians are picked up and moved by storms—it might not rain cats and dogs, but it can rain frogs and toads); it might make a hitchhiker's journey on the back of a swimming mammal, or on the feet of a migrating bird; or it might use transportation provided by humans, both intentional and unintentional.

Large mammals like the bear and the deer can cross the open waters by swimming. I watched a deer swim across my bow as I sailed between Red Cliff and Basswood Island. The deer swam in a straight line and appeared intent on the island. What caused it to go into the water could have been any number of things: being chased by a predator, seeking refuge from biting insects, or simply wandering. I have seen deer walk into a lake to drink and keep going, as though they didn't want to turn around.

The deer can also cross the ice during the winter, along with coyote and fox, but the bear that inhabit the islands have to come over by swimming, since they winter sleep when the ice cover is thick.

In addition to the problem of crossing the water barriers, the ecology of wildlife is also dependent on the plant life that is available for nesting and foraging. We know very little about the insects of the Apostles. There has not been sufficient study to determine their ecology, but certainly the plants and the habitats for insects determine some of the food for the birds. Since the majority of insects can be transported through flight, there seems to be very little to deter their spread on the islands, other than suitable places to reproduce and the proper food plants.

The limits of food are a major consideration for the large mammals like the deer and the bear. There were large populations of deer on Rocky and Bear islands in 1954, but a food shortage caused an almost complete die-off in the early sixties. When deer reach the islands, their favorite food is the Canada yew, an evergreen shrub that can dominate the understory of some islands when there is no grazing to prune it back. The absence of yew is a good indicator of too many deer. The removal of yew by browsing increased the sugar maple and the mountain maple populations on Rocky Island. Hemlock and cedar also disappeared on Rocky due to browsing.

Only two of the islands had human communities, though the others had isolated human groups—it is a good analogy for the plant communities, too. Often size is a factor in diversity. Islands like North Twin, South Twin, and Devils tend to be limited in community structures—they are just too small to host a variety of plant communities.

All the different communities on the islands are grouped into five major types, which are dune, northern coniferous forest, northern mixed forest, shrub carr, and open bog. The first four types are all found on Oak. Oak Island is the most diverse because it is large in circumference and height. The old beach lines from ancient lake levels create areas of drainage that are different from the clay soil that dominates most of the islands and the majority of Oak. These well-drained soils support the oak trees that give the island its name and provide food for blue jays, white-tailed deer, bear, wood duck, and squirrels. Deep ravines on Oak Island have eroded into the thick clay sediments. These create steep slopes that dry if they face south and are exposed to the sun, or stay moist and cool if they face north. At the bottom of the ravines are streams that support different life, including native brook trout, which spawn near the campsite on the northeast beach. Finally, Oak has a sandspit community.

Oak has also been affected by systematic logging since 1871 and by a major fire in 1943. Most of the islands have had similar factors in their history.

Outer Island is the most removed from the mainland, and that affects its composition. Some organisms don't move as well as others. The large sandspit on Outer provides some very special elements and adds species that are absent from the other islands. Large spits usually develop from two side sandbars that extend from the island until they are of sufficient length to unite. In the uniting, a portion of the lake that existed between the sandbars can be trapped. This leaves a wetland—bogs on Raspberry and Rocky, and bog lakes on Outer and Michigan.

The biggest lake is on Outer, and it supports loons and other waterfowl, as well as a population of northern pike. The pike are stunted because of their confined home territory, and this stunted growth indicates that they are in fact an isolated population, which has been altered by its home. The lagoon also supports the central mudminnow, a small fish that is probably the prime food of the northern.

The convergence of the two spits actually creates an environment with twelve different plant communities. The ecologist lists them as dune grass area (this grass is an endangered species in Wisconsin and is important in holding the sand from erosion), sedge hollow, beach heather community, pine and blueberry area (the best blueberries in the islands), pine/bracken fern area (just a little older version of the last community), black spruce forest, pine/birch forest, pines and maples, hemlock and birch, leatherleaf and pine, sedge in sphagnum, and sedge/sphagnum area with blueberries. Many of these communities are successional stages of others; but they often exist at the same time on the same spit, and each one has just a little different animal and plant composition.

The eroded clay valleys on Outer have beaver streams. There were at least forty-six active beaver colonies on Outer at one time. The beaver ponds support good alder thickets, and these in turn support good migratory populations of woodcock. These wetlands also support weasel, muskrat, and one small species of fish—the brook stickleback.

Outer Island has one of the more unusual bird migration patterns in the region. The north-flying birds move through the islands and over the channels, as though the islands are part of the mainland. Then they reach the big lake and hesitate. Except for crossing the gulf of Mexico, most small birds try to avoid large open-water areas, where they are vulnerable to storms and predation. Lake Superior represents a very large obstacle. During May the birds keep coming out to the island and stopping, until it is a deluxe aviary filled to overflowing. Eventually it is too full and the urge to go north is too strong. One observer watched more than two thousand birds exit the sandspit, going south one May night. Presumably they hit the mainland and move around the lake near Duluth.

Reptiles and amphibians are part of the island ecology, but their distribution is erratic. The four-toed salamander, for instance, is on Michigan, Outer, South Twin, and Raspberry—at least, that is all it has been found on. Why those four?

Why?—the driving question in ecological study. The islands of Sand, Outer, Devils, Raspberry, York, and North Twin have never known the large deer herds that have devasted the yew population on the other islands. When you look at a map of the islands, it is difficult to see why this combination was missed.

Mollusks—clams and snails—have very little diversity in the Apostles, only 20 percent of the diversity of the Mississippi River and 40 percent of Isle Royale's. Snails are found on most islands, but the clams seem confined to the inland lagoons, which leads a person to wonder how they got there in the first place. Three species that are not currently found were discovered in archaeological digs. They could have been brought there from other locations for use by the Indians, or their presence could indicate a different climatic/lake condition in the past, or it could indicate their extirpation.

Moose were eliminated from the area by a disease that is transmitted through white-tailed deer. They were gone from the entire state by 1921. Wolves were also extirpated from the state and have just recently begun to reestablish themselves. Some are close enough that they might visit the Apostles in the future. Pine marten and fisher were also eliminated, but reintroduction efforts have been successful in the Chequamegon National Forest. The state of Wisconsin released martens on Stockton Island in 1953 and 1956, but it appears that those efforts failed.

An unusual bird, the capercaillie (Swedish uhr hen), was introduced to Outer Island as a game bird by the Wisconsin Conservation Department in 1949, but fortunately it was gone by 1951. The introduction of species like the uhr hen can be very destructive to native populations. The house sparrow and the starling are good examples of destructive introductions. So far they have not prospered on the islands. Humans have brought in one organism that can be even more devastating—purple loosestrife. This beautiful devil of a plant can choke the life out of our wetlands. Human change can spawn a complex chain of events in the wilds.

White-tailed deer. (D. Cox)

Red squirrel. (D. Cox)

Sharptailed grouse were abundant on Stockton after a fire, but the regrowth of the forest eliminated them. They represent a transitory population that took advantage of a temporary condition. In many ways deer were the same way, finding human activities—logging and agriculture—beneficial to their spread. For the deer, these conditions have persisted and allowed them to be considered a part of the natural composition of the land.

There are more "why" species. The eastern grey squirrel immigrated to the area with the logging and change in forest composition, but unlike the red squirrel it has not made it out to the islands. Of course, even the red squirrel finds limits in the island ecology. Their density is less than on the mainland and is restricted to the conifer forests.

The striped skunk, woodchuck, porcupine, raccoon, eastern chipmunk, and least chipmunk are all abundant on the mainland and absent in the islands. They all are hibernators or have minimum winter movement. The raccoon has been a recent addition to the northern forests and could possibly swim across. If it gets onto one of the bird-nesting islands, it could have a devastating impact. Jumping mice and flying squirrels are mammals that also have not made the crossing, as yet.

The park staff is conscious of the ecological significance of the island; the reporting of unusual phenomena is stronger now than in the past and more research is going on now than ever before. We know that sandhill cranes laid eggs for three years on Stockton but raised no young, we know that common loons had an unsuccessful nesting in 1985, and we know that merlins had a successful nest on Stockton in 1987.

This scientific work will enhance the visitors' experience and should help in the protection of the natural environments. These investigations are important for monitoring the health of the islands. The preservation of the natural ecosystems is the Park Service's number-one responsibility.

Sandhill cranes have nested in this bog on Stockton Island. (J. and A. Mahan)

Tree swallows nesting inside a sea cave on Oak Island. (P. Chalfant)

THE FALL OF THE HEMLOCKS

The breath of the earth was cold as it plunged down from the glaciers and swept across the newly exposed landscape. Warmer air blew across the grasslands and the new forests to the south and west, while short tundra plants eked out survival on the permafrost of Bayfield and Ashland counties. Removal of the ice mass to the north moderated the climate, and spruce parklands and spruce/fir combinations dotted the peninsula, like the northern boreal forests of today.

Seven thousand years ago the forests took on more diversity, and jack pine and red pine grew on the drier, more fire-prone uplands and the old sandy beachlines. Up to the time of modern Lake Superior, about four thousand years ago, white pine dominated the region—it would have been a logger's dream. The fires that maintained the pine lands became less frequent, and the climate became colder and moister along the south shore, giving us the current conifer/hardwoods mix. It was a hemlock–yellow birch–white pine complex, a transitional forest between the southern deciduous forest and the northern boreal biome.

When the traders first came to the islands they found a dense stand of hardwoods and hemlocks with giant white pines towering above them. It was a forest that had known succession only through fire, wind, insect damage, and age. But the winds of human change blew in from the north like the winds off the glaciers.

In 1857, the forests were still virtually untouched, according to the notes that accompanied the land office surveys, but many factors contributed to the removal of the forest. In some ways the spread of logging was a steady progression across the state, moving up the waterways, following the courses that would transport the logger to the cut and the trees to the mill. It was a water industry of sluiceways and dams.

The Apostles moved ahead of some of the northern forests in the sequence of harvest because of their special location. Chequamegon Bay was a natural millpond. Streams entered it from two directions, and the lake came in from a third. The streams could aid the mainland harvest in the normal sequence of cutting, but the lake was a more dependable transportation corridor and gave the logger access to farther, more lucrative ports.

Mills were established in Bayfield, Washburn, and Ashland, but Duluth and other port cities could also buy the products of the islands. The big pines were natural targets since the timber industry had been primarily a white-pine industry and the East had already been too heavily logged. The islands were like a new mineral strike.

On the islands, the timber could be cut and dragged to the Lake, where the pines were floated to the mainland. On the mainland, the trees were skidded to an intermediary point where they were loaded and hauled to a landing for floating to the mill. On Rocky Island, Nicholas Rabideaux, a descendant of an American Fur Company employee, logged 350,000 board feet of pine in 1897. Two million board feet were taken from Bass Island that same year.

The island locations also provided another advantage to the logger. Pines were preferred because they would float, not because they were better lumber. Hardwoods would sink too quickly for river transport. In the islands, where barges could come right up to the shore, the hardwoods could also be harvested.

The timber that left the islands had many uses; Bayfield was a winter storehouse of cordwood, sawlogs, pilings, posts, poles, and shingles. There was a barrel cooperage, and there were piles of hemlock bark for the tannery. In addition, the lumber industry supported two other industries. The iron mines in Wisconsin and Michigan used the logs for shafts and tunnels as well as mine and townsite buildings. The major consumer was also the major transporter—the railroad. The country was a vast network of iron, spread across 125,000 board feet of lumber per mile. In addition, the locomotives burned timber, and it was used for bridges, buildings, docks, and tunnels.

The hemlock forests were harvested for their bark.

On Rocky Island, a trail takes hikers deep into an old maple/yellow birch forest. (K. Crowley)

Later the wood was utilized as well, but the initial years saw the big virgin hemlocks dropped onto beds of smaller trees and boughs. Then the bark was split and removed. The harvest was for tannic acid, the natural dye that colors tree bark. The leather industry required tannin for "tanning" hides.

On the islands, dry sluiceways were built, steep chutes that depended on gravity rather than water for transport, and the shinglelike hunks of bark were sent downhill to the shipping point. The prime months for hemlock harvest were May to July, the months when most other logging was at a standstill.

Logging underwent a series of adjustments that extended the industry's life. After the pines came the hemlocks and hardwood veneer harvesting, and later there was a second wave of veneer harvesting and pulpwood. William Knight on Oak Island ran an ad for a large supply of dry hardwood and hemlock at his dock. Much of the Oak Island wood supplied the steamship boilers. No island escaped the saw and axe except for Gull, and possibly Eagle, although North Twin, Raspberry, and Devils were not logged commercially.

Michigan and Outer Islands were logged by railroad, some islands had heavy equipment, and many islands had lumber camps. These resident areas were all over Oak Island, and Lullaby Camp on Outer Island did not close until 1952. Today you can walk through the remains of this island lumber camp. There are old buildings among the new-growth forest, the smooth wood of the double-seated outhouse, and rusting machinery. The landscape has been altered here, but the forest is reclaiming the spot.

Logging is part of the legacy of the park, but it is also a factor in the ecology. On Outer Island there is still a virgin hemlock stand. This is rare even beyond the islands, and it points out one of the major effects of logging. The hemlock trees flower from April to June, depending on the seasonal conditions, and they produce a good seed stock once every two to three years. In order to reproduce, the seeds require a constant high humidity, but the logging and the fires that followed created a warmer, dryer island habitat. Increased exposure dried the seeds, increased sunscald on seedlings, and encouraged insect infestation. Also, H. A. Godes found that in natural reproduction, most seedlings were on old pine and hemlock logs. These were not available after logging. In many cases sugar maples have taken the hemlocks' place in the forest composition.

In other areas, aspen and paper birch have crowded out the yellow birch and pines. Introduced plants and animals (rodents and insects) compete with the native plants and often eliminate them.

The forests of today are rich and green; they look natural and wild until we look closer at the ancient stumps and the records of trees logged. We find hemlock that looks young according to its size, but research shows that it is old-growth hemlock that has been stunted by a combination of factors.

The three-hundred-year-old pines on Sand Island are a reminder of the giants that once rose above all the forests. Now the park planners must decide what is natural, what is optimal, and what is possible. It is a tough decision, and there are no guarantees no matter what they choose.

In Bayfield, a historic cooperage still produces the wooden barrels that once were used to pack and ship salted fish.
(D. Albrecht)

In Bayfield, a historic cooperage still produces the wooden barrels that once were used to pack and ship salted fish. (D. Albrecht)

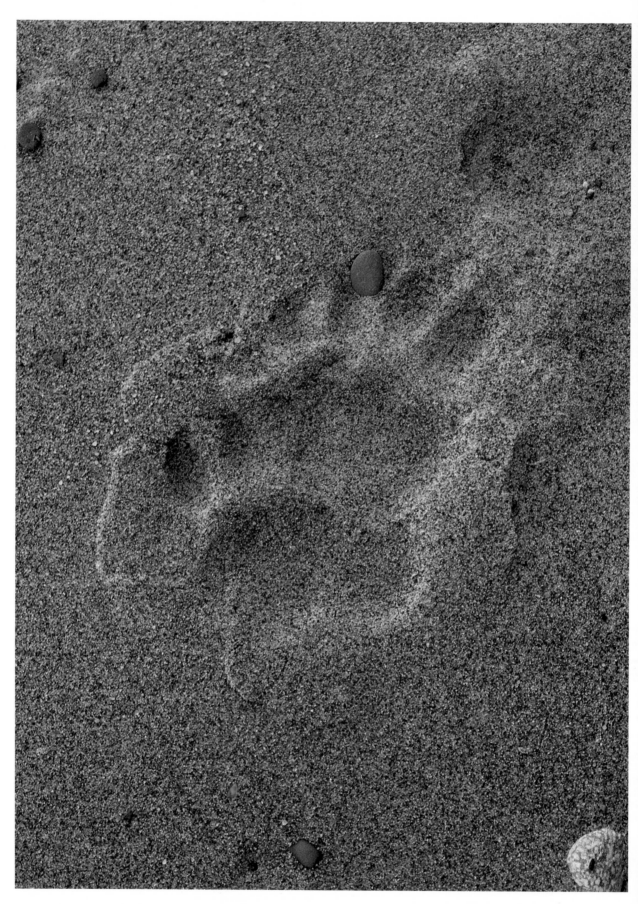

Bear tracks on an Oak Island beach. (P. Chalfant)

BEAVERS
AND BEARS

In nature, nothing is static. Numbers rise and fall. Species appear and disappear. The Apostle Islands have seen great changes during their formation and continued existence, including the number and variety of wildlife that has lived there.

The more technology humans develop or bring with them, the more significant is the impact. On the positive side, increased knowledge that accompanies the improved technologies can work for the understanding and betterment of wildlife.

Wildlife numbers are significant, but always changing. The figures recorded in these pages will probably be inaccurate by the time this information is published. We record them here to be used as a comparison for people in years to come. The story never ends, unless a species becomes extinct.

★   ★   ★

Two of the large mammals found on the islands are the beaver and the black bear. Because they are confined to their dens and lodges during the winter months, it must be assumed that they got to the islands during the months when they could swim from the mainland and then "island hop" as the need arose.

BEAVER (*ah-mik* in Ojibwa)

The beaver played a very large role in the settlement of these islands. In the 1700s, felt hats were the rage in Europe, and the beaver had the best pelt for making the hats. When French explorers entered the Great Lakes region and traded with the Indians, the beaver were plentiful. One estimate put their numbers in the hundreds of millions.

Before long, a vigorous fur trade was established. The romantic character of the voyageur—gregarious, robust, song-loving—grew out of the beaver trade. The first settlement in Wisconsin, the village of La Pointe on Madeline Island, was established in 1693 by Pierre Le Sueur. An archaeological dig site on Madeline unearthed large quantities of beaver bones.

Eventually the beaver hats went out of style, and the beaver almost did too. They were wiped out of southern Wisconsin by 1825 and most of the state by 1900. Luckily some of these large rodents were missed, and in the 1920s excess beavers were trapped and moved to locations where they had been eliminated. Today, experts estimate there are approximately two million in the United States.

The beavers that lived on the Bayfield peninsula prior to the arrival of the fur trade were making a living in areas of forest that had been burned over (the Brule River was originally *Bois Brulé*, which translates to "burnt wood"). A regenerating forest provides their favorite food—young aspen trees.

Once the fur trade died out, a new wave of exploitation arrived in the Apostle Islands—the logging era. This was before the days of forest management, and the new goal was to cut as many trees as possible. Countless species of wildlife lost their homes and sources of food. The ground was exposed to erosion, and water ran off rather than following the usual pattern of soil absorption. But this provided the beaver with the kind of young forest it thrives on.

In the Apostle Islands National Lakeshore today, Outer and Stockton islands, the two largest islands in the park, have the greatest numbers of beaver. Stockton, the larger, is a fairly low island that includes a small lagoon. Outer Island is much more elevated, with a large amount of natural drainage, as well as a small lagoon on its southeastern end.

Sandy Sharp spent a summer as a volunteer lighthouse keeper on Outer Island, where she could get away from the stress and fast pace of city life while learning more about herself, Lake Superior, and the Apostle Islands. The volunteer lighthouse keepers serve as representatives of the National Park Service. They greet visitors to the islands, and live in and help maintain the structures that still stand. The house on Outer Island is a big, old, rambling, two-story, brick building. It is structurally sound, but has not been remodeled to meet modern standards, which means that the toilet facilities are still out back.

It was Sandy's habit to get up in the morning, get a pot of coffee going, and if there were no visitors at the house, make a morning visit to the outhouse. One such morning, still in her nightgown and somewhat bleary-eyed, she caught a glimpse of a furry, brown animal ambling across the yard. She thought to herself, "Hmm, someone's dog . . . " Since she hadn't had her morning shot of caffeine yet, her brain wasn't completely in gear. But a moment later, she stopped, did a double take, and said, "Wait a minute—there aren't any dogs out here!" As she turned to look, a very fat and unconcerned beaver waddled over to an aspen tree to check it out as a possible breakfast item. Dissatisfied, it left the yard and rambled back to its dam, which was not too far up the trail from the lighthouse.

Sandy had frequent sightings of beavers as she made her weekly walks on the island trails. If she came up quietly on the flowages, the beavers would continue to swim or work on their dams. On one trip, she came onto a flowage where a confrontation between two beavers was underway. One beaver was repeatedly slapping its tail on the water, while the other swam and dove. It wasn't a warning slap, because neither disappeared. It may have been an adult trying to convince a youngster that it was time to leave home and find a flowage of its own.

Beavers are engineers who alter a landscape almost as dramatically as humans do. They gravitate to streams, where they can build a dam, causing water to back up and form their own personal reservoir. This allows them to have easier access to food trees and a protected place to build their lodge and store food for the winter.

As the stream backs up, forest land is flooded, trees die, silt is deposited on the bottom, and, over a long period of time, the pond gradually fills in and forms a new meadowland. However, beavers cannot distinguish between trees that we wish to preserve and those we care less about. In more recent times, they have come into conflict with people because of their arbitrary choices for dam building and tree sampling. In suburban areas and certain rural regions, homeowners have suffered land and ornamental tree loss because of the beavers' persistence once they've chosen a site for their home.

On Outer Island, beavers have been a major influential factor since the mid-1960s, when the impact of both logging and fires left them with an ideal habitat. A 1938 aerial photo shows no beaver colonies on Outer, but now nearly all the drainage patterns on the island have been occupied and altered. On the northern portion of the island, white cedar, hemlock, and yellow birch trees have died because of flooding from beaver dams. On the southern end of the island, white birch have suffered a similar fate.

Researchers have studied the beavers on Outer Island and found that their food preferences among the woody plants, in descending order, were trembling aspen, pin cherry, willow, yellow birch, mountain ash, sugar maple, mountain maple, red maple, white birch, and white cedar. The trees they chose most often had a diameter of 2.5 to 7.6 cm.

In the summer, the beavers showed a preference for leafy and aquatic plants and moved from pond to pond within the same flowages to feed. By October, their feeding was more localized around the area where they would overwinter, and the cutting of woody species increased. The woody plant material is their major source of food in winter, although there have been some reports of beavers eating yellow water lilies in the winter.

On Outer Island, beavers really have no predators to fear—but in most other places, the farther a beaver travels from its stream or pond, the greater are its chances of attack by a wolf, bobcat, or lynx.

In the 1978 study of beavers on Outer Island, there were thirty-three families and thirteen single or pair colonies counted. Deeper flowages supported families through the winter, but it is doubtful that those in shallow (less than one meter deep) ponds are able to survive winter. Young beavers, after spending two years with their parents, are forced to leave the home pond and seek their own fortunes. In a restricted area, such as an island, a youngster may be forced to take marginal habitat or leave altogether. The number of beavers in a single colony can vary depending on food conditions, but generally there are two parents and two to four young.

Chances of seeing a beaver on the islands are slim for the occasional visitor, since beavers tend to live away from the shorelines, and vegetation can be thick away from the trails. But you may be fortunate, as we were one early evening in August on Madeline Island. Just across the street from the marina is a waterway that connects Superior to an old bog. A small bridge passes over the water. As we walked at dusk, we caught sight of two dark shapes with wedge-shaped heads, cutting through the water. Too small for beavers, we thought—must be muskrats. But we stopped and watched awhile. The two forms had stopped to feed on some green stalks growing out of the water.

We tried to distinguish the tail shapes, but the angle and low level of light didn't give us a very good view. Then swimming out of the bog came a larger dark shape, and as it neared the two smaller ones, a loud "whack" came from the water and the two small animals dove from sight. Momma beaver had come looking for her wayward youngsters and answered our question. We watched as the two young ones reappeared and swam dutifully back to the bog with their mother following close behind.

BLACK BEAR (*muk-wa* in Ojibwa)

Our boat was tied to the Stockton dock one morning, and as I emerged from the cabin, I noticed Ranger Paul Chalfant standing at the end of the dock, wearing a pair of headphones and pointing a metal T-shaped device at the other end of the island. I recognized it as a radio-tracking antenna that wildlife researchers use

Beaver. (D. Cox)

Black Bear cubs. (D. Cox)

to locate radio-collared animals. I walked down to him, and as he took off his headphones, I asked what he was trying to find.

"There's a female bear we've collared that's been wandering around over there."

Some of our crew members had arrived at the boat by this time, and they came down to see what was going on. Paul let those who were interested put the headphones on, and showed them how to hold the antenna and listen for an increase in the intensity of beeps, indicating the bear was in range. It was a good chance for our group to get some firsthand understanding of a portion of a researcher's job. They also learned something about the black bears that live on Stockton Island.

Bears are land animals, but they have been observed swimming from one island to the next. Some bears may come to the islands in the summer and then go back to the mainland in the fall, just as many people do. Other bears have found the food on the islands abundant enough to allow them to live there throughout the year. They have been found on Stockton, Oak, Raspberry, Ironwood, Michigan, Sand, and Manitou islands.

The islands produce an assortment of berries and nuts — bears' prime food sources — but the island bears are subsisting in smaller territories compared to their counterparts in mainland Wisconsin and in Canada. According to a study done in 1984, the female bear on Stockton had a range of 13 square kilometers, while the male had a range of 20 square kilometers. The mainland and Canadian females' territories were 19 and 20 square kilometers; the males' were 93 and 120 square kilometers!

Some islands are more bountiful than others. One bear that was found dead on Ironwood Island the winter of 1986–87 was in very poor condition. The bears studied on Stockton, when trapped, weighed 133 pounds and 190 pounds (female and male respectively). These weights are fairly low for black bears. But these factors don't seem to be inhibiting the growth of the population.

The University of Wisconsin at Stevens Point has radio-collared bears to try to obtain more information on their movements both on and between the islands. During the winter months, researchers locate the bear dens and change the batteries on the collars. It also gives them a chance to assess the animals' health.

In the past, there have been so few bears on any of the islands that there was little contact between them and humans. Now more people are visiting and camping on Stockton Island, and it appears the bear population has grown. In the summer of 1987, a radio-collared bear visited the Presque Isle group campground in search of food. She was one of eight or nine bears on Stockton Island, four of whom were radio collared. Two of the bears were cubs, born on the island. Another bear has been seen in the campground on Oak Island.

Stockton Island receives the greatest amount of visitorship in the summer, and because of the good crop of blueberries that draws both people and bears, the chances of encountering a bear are growing. Sandy, our lighthouse keeper friend, had this advice: "If you're blueberry picking on Stockton, and you come upon a very large pile of partially digested blueberries, you can be pretty sure that you're not the only one who has found the patch."

Black bears by and large are not any more interested in a close encounter with us than we are with them. They are naturally shy and will retreat quickly if given a chance. But it must always be remembered that they are wild and sometimes unpredictable. Bears have personalities too, and though we try to calm people's fears of coming across a bear, we also suggest caution and reasonable behavior, especially in the campgrounds. Don't keep food of any sort in your tent — bears have a very good sense of smell, and a zipper-type plastic bag lets molecules of odor escape. If you have food in a pack, it is best to hoist it up on a branch, a good fifteen feet off the ground. This isn't a guarantee that a bear won't get it — they can be very creative and persistent — but it may discourage them. Don't leave food scraps lying around, on, or under picnic tables, even if you like to watch the squirrels come in and stuff their cute little cheeks. You may attract an unwanted visitor.

The Park Service has monitored the increase in bears and is now working on a management plan so that visitors can continue to use and enjoy the islands and the bears can continue to live there in peace as well.

An old beaver dam on Outer Island. (J. and A. Mahan)

46

Wilson's warbler. (D. Cox)

BIRDS
OF THE ISLANDS

Little is known of the wildlife in the Apostle Islands before this century. Serious scientific study was undertaken in the 1940s and 1950s, but with the inclusion of the Apostle Islands in the National Park system in 1970, the number of studies has increased dramatically—all islands are now inventoried for bird species.

What we know of bird life on the islands in earlier times comes from notes made by the explorers and settlers. In the late 1600s, French explorer Radisson camped near the head of Chequamegon Bay and reported seeing "a good store of bustards" (swans or geese). Passenger pigeons (which became extinct in 1914) may have used the islands as a stopping point during their crossings of Lake Superior. The islands do serve as a much needed resting spot for birds that are migrating across the great expanse of water that separates Canadian breeding grounds from their winter southern ranges.

Over one hundred species of nesting birds have been counted in the Apostle Islands, but of these, only about twelve species will stay all year. The mixed coniferous/deciduous forest allows diversity of bird species on even the smaller islands.

An island visitor is more likely to hear the small birds sing than to see them in the dense forest cover. The only open ground is the sandy beach or rocky ledge that separates the forest edge from the water. The most frequently observed birds are species that are closely tied to the water for their survival.

PIPING PLOVER

A relative of the killdeer, the piping plover is only six inches long, with a light sandy-colored back, a white breast, and a single dark brown band around its neck. The lack of distinguishing features camouflages the plover when you look for it on a long stretch of beach that has little vegetation but lots of pebbles, shells, and other beach refuse. Even when you hear its high pitched "peep," you may still search vainly. Only the

bird's movement seems to allow the observer to spot it.

Never abundant in the Great Lakes, the plovers have dwindled drastically in the past eighty years. In 1900, an estimated 140 adults nested along the shores of the lake and on island beaches. In 1986, it was believed that only two pairs bred in the same area. During summer of 1987, a few stray adults were seen, but no nests were discovered.

The piping plover has been waging a losing battle over its nesting territories—sandy beaches with little human disturbance. In the Great Lakes alone, there are 10,000 miles of shoreline that could be potential nesting areas, but there are only five miles left where the birds can nest without disturbance. Directly and indirectly, we humans are causing this little beach bum of a bird to disappear. Shorelines are going under condos, all-terrain vehicles, and beach towels. Our management of the lake levels and mismanagement of the land are causing the water to creep up the beachline, pushing the plovers even further back.

In the Apostles, Long Island is the only spot in all Wisconsin where the birds have been known to breed. Long Island is a narrow strip of sand that alternates from peninsula to island, depending on weather conditions. Although it still contains a lighthouse, it receives few visitors.

Piping plover nests are single shallow scrapes in the sand, lined with pebbles, shells, or driftwood. The three to five eggs are so perfectly camouflaged with the sand that one could search for hours and not find the nest. The only clue that a nest exists would be the behavior of the worried parent bird. Like their cousin the killdeer, they perform the broken-wing act when a predator (two-legged or four-legged) approaches.

In 1974, a breeding project began in the Apostle Islands. In May 1981 a pair of piping plovers nested on the northeastern tip of Long Island and laid four eggs. Another pair was seen on the southeastern tip of the island, but no nest was found. Researchers returned to the island in early July and found the tracks of skunk,

Overleaf: Great blue heron. (D. Cox)

bear, and dirt bike, as well as a dead fox—but they found no sign of any piping plovers. Some of the bike tracks came within five to six meters of the nest scrape. It was impossible to say what was the exact cause for the absence of the birds. The clues indicated it could have been predation by other animals, human disturbance, or a combination of the two. It is also possible, but unlikely, that the adult birds and their young fledged and migrated early.

Although the outlook isn't good for the piping plover, the Park Service has not given up hope. There is currently a study being done through the University of Minnesota to analyze the habitat needs and food requirements of the piping plovers on Long Island and in three other parks in the Great Lakes. It is hoped that the results will indicate what needs to be done to find a way for the piping plovers to once again nest and raise young in the Apostle Islands.

GREAT BLUE HERON

Watching a great blue heron walking/stalking in shallow water, you almost become hypnotized by the sinuous, snakelike neck. In a relaxed pose, the neck is S-shaped, but herons are fishing birds that can straighten their neck in the flash of a second, enabling their sharp bayonetlike beak to grab big fish swimming in shallow water. (If you ever come upon an injured bird, approach with great caution. They have excellent aim and seem to target the eyes. One bird was known to strike and pierce a wooden oar so hard that two inches of bill stuck through the other side.) Small fish are grabbed crosswise in the bill, and all food is gulped down whole.

While the majority of their prey are fish, they will eat reptiles, insects, and even small mammals. Preferring to feed at dawn or dusk, herons move from one island to the next and have been observed on thirteen of the Apostles, including Eagle, their nesting island.

The great blue stands about four feet tall, with a wingspread of seven feet, making it the largest heron in North America. It balances on long, black, stiltlike legs, and its feathers appear more grayish than blue, with white feathers around the head and neck, a black skullcap, and touches of cinnamon down the long neck.

In flight, a great blue heron beats its big wings in slow cadence, flying with neck tucked back and legs extended out behind. If startled into flight, they might croak, but usually the only sound is the rhythmic whoosh of air being pushed down by long feathered wings.

A heron rookery is a picture out of prehistoric times. In the bare, bent branches of the dying trees stand birds that remind me of the fossil bird, archaeopteryx. The voice of the great blue heron is a harsh, guttural squawk, and a nesting colony will be filled with a cacophony of young birds on the nest and adult birds flying in with food. The discordant sounds carry a long way out over the water.

Eagle Island, the most westerly of the Apostles, may have once been home to eagles. Its twenty-eight acres are covered with a mixed forest of white and yellow birch, fir, and spruce. A rocky shoreline circles the island, and just offshore lie dangerous submerged shoals. The heron rookery was first reported in 1972. Since the mid-1950s, when the State of Wisconsin began to make periodic surveys of heron rookeries, there has been a noticeable decrease in the southern part of the state, while the northwest and north central regions seem to be showing an increase in the number of colonies.

On Eagle, great blue herons nest in the upper branches of the dead and dying yellow birch trees. Often one tree will be decorated with five to twelve nests, depending on available branches. The nests are haphazard-looking piles of sticks, which are reused year after year, with minor modifications made by the new owners. Some old nests can extend three to four feet across, while new ones may be only eighteen inches across.

The herons begin to return to the Apostles in late March, and egg laying begins soon afterward. The male gathers sticks and passes them to the female, who arranges them. During the early breeding season, the birds are especially sensitive to human disturbance and will vacate their nests if approached. As the breeding season progresses, they are less quick to leave the nest, but Park rules prohibit people from approaching closer than one hundred yards to any of the nesting islands between the months of May and August.

Until 1985, the herons had to share their island only with the herring gulls, who built their nests on the rocks. But in recent years, double-crested cormorants have managed to get a foothold, literally, on some of the trees that the herons have used for nesting. At first there were only a dozen, but each year the numbers have grown. It is not unusual to find herons and cormorants nesting in the same trees.

There are many questions regarding the Apostle Island herons: Will the cormorants continue to put pressure on the heron rookery? What will happen when the yellow birch trees finally succumb to weather? Will the herons be able to find other suitable trees in the islands or will they have to abandon their island retreat for life on the mainland?

HERRING GULL

No other bird conjures up images of salt spray and waves as quickly as a gull. Away from the water, their squeaky calls are harsh on the ears, but in their element they blend with the creaking of hulls and clanging of rigging.

In the Apostle Islands, the gulls are the most abundant and conspicuous birds, with an entire island named for them. In the late 1800s, Sam S. Fifield described two gull rookeries in the Apostle Islands. One was Gull Island and the other was Little Manitou Island, which no longer exists—the Coast Guard washed it away with high powered water hoses in 1948 (all that remains is a small pile of rocks that sup-

Ring-billed gulls. (D. Cox)

Young double-crested cormorants in their nests on Gull Island. (D. Cox)

ports a navigational light and a small gathering of gulls and cormorants).

Gulls are highly visible colonial ground nesters, and as such may act as an early warning system for adverse changes in the environment. Their sensitivity to environmental changes makes them an ecological indicator for the Lake Superior region. Herring gulls have been noticably affected by the chemicals DDE and PCB. In 1974, some of their eggs were collected on Gull Island, and the shells were found to be 7 percent thinner than normal.

In 1984, herring gulls were nesting on Gull, Eagle, Otter, Bear, Outer, Hermit, Cat, Little Manitou, Devils, and Sand Islands. The number of nesting pairs had increased by 29 percent in ten years. While the herring gull population grew, the smaller, less aggressive ring-billed gulls diminished. No nesting by ring-billed gulls has been seen in the islands for several years (the 1974 survey showed only ten to twenty pairs), but adult birds are still seen in small numbers, especially around Bayfield.

Gull Island, the major nesting island, is the smallest of the Apostles (if you don't count Little Manitou). It lies off the northwestern tip of Michigan Island and is connected to its bigger neighbor by a shallow rock reef. Barely above lake level, it is an island of pebbles and stone, with a scattered growth of blue grass, red elderberry, and mountain maple. Exposure to wind and waves makes it difficult for vegetation to get a good grip on the rocky soil.

A tall navigational tower makes the little island look like a fishing boat from the distance, an illusion that is intensified by a fish odor as you approach. Double-crested cormorants share the island with the gulls, and as you get closer you see the salt and pepper colors of the colony and you hear the birds' squawks and calls. Gull Island is much whiter than the other islands because of the accumulated guano of thousands of birds and decades of use.

It is a relatively safe place to raise young because the lack of vegetation on the island provides no hiding place for predators. Herring gulls that choose to nest outside of a colony, on the rock cliffs along a forest edge, are probably much less successful in raising young due to the increased chance of predation.

Gulls are associated with both large bodies of water and garbage. They are born scavengers. Within a twenty-five-mile radius of Bayfield, there are five state-approved garbage dumps—another reason for gulls' large numbers in the islands. If the fishing is poor, they just head to their supplemental feeding grounds. They have been cleaning up after humans for as long as the two have existed in the same areas.

Their habit of scavenging scraps makes them easy targets for bribery. Out on the water we watch as a fishing boat appears in the distance, accompanied by a swirling cloud of bright white flecks. Even though we cannot see the fishermen cleaning their catch and tossing the remains overboard, we know of their activity by watching the gulls. They fly close to the boat, then veer up and drop back into the water to feast on fish entrails. The boat powers ahead, leaving a white wake of curling waves and fat herring gulls. Some gulls tire of the fly/feed routine and catch a ride on the roof of the fishing boat.

One day, after watching a fishing vessel pass with its entourage of gulls, I decided to toss some crumbs to see if I could entice the birds our way. It must've been a slow day on the fishing boat, because first one gull peeled off and over to our boat, and then another followed, and another, and before long we were being followed by our own cloud of white. The birds not only flew and dove around us and after the bread crumbs, they noisily argued over rights to each piece of bread.

There is something wonderful about moving forward and watching these birds keep pace with you, with so little effort. Often times, if the wind is blowing right, they simply set their wings, change the angle of them slightly, and continue to move forward. Their aerobatic ability and apparent freedom from gravity fill me with envy. When the crumbs fall no more, the gulls drop behind and wait for another opportunity to appear.

I was so inspired by my success in enticing the birds that on future days whenever I would see some gulls nearby, I would rush below for some scrap to lure them to us. More often they ignored my pleas and dramatic flings of the arm; but on a few occasions I would draw in one bird, and then, as if forming from the clouds above, birds would begin to wing in one at a time. Whether they came from the islands or were sitting on the water, I could never tell.

When boats anchor in a protected bay at night, almost always one or two gulls patrol the water around the hulls. Years of experience have taught them that eventually food will come from these movable islands.

It was a midsummer evening and we were anchored in Julian Bay (off Stockton Island). The moon was rising in a still blue sky and the sun was setting behind the bog, throwing up a curtain of golden pink light. Mike and I were on the deck listening to music that was drifting up from the cabin below. We felt inspired to dance slowly across our private, floating ballroom. A more romantic setting would be hard to find. We didn't even care if other boaters looked at us askance—but our spell was broken by the jeering laugh of a herring gull that swam a few feet away. I made disparaging remarks at it, but then others joined in and continued to ridicule us. The mood was not ruined though, for I decided that this time the gulls were jealous of us.

DOUBLE-CRESTED CORMORANT

Probably the most controversial animal living in the Apostle Islands is the double-crested cormorant. Commercial fishermen see these birds as direct competitors for their livelihood—the fish of Lake Superior. Prior to the twentieth century, cormorants were abundant in the Great Lakes, as were the fish they depended on.

The fisherman's war on cormorants peaked between

1920 and 1945, when the fisheries industry boomed. The combination of overfishing and the introduction of lamprey (through the Saint Lawrence seaway), which preyed on the commercial fish, destroyed the industry. Between the 1950s and the 1970s, the introduction of harmful chemicals to the lakes, as well as other human-related disturbances, caused the numbers of cormorants to drop, and they were listed as endangered in Wisconsin in 1972.

During the mid-1970s, the fish returned and the protection and management of the cormorants allowed their numbers to recover. By the mid-1980s, their population had reached sufficient size to change their status from endangered to threatened.

Double-crested cormorants get their name for two fairly inconspicuous tufts of feathers that appear on the crown briefly, during the breeding season. Other, older names for the bird are "shag" and, for some reason, "lawyer." Both male and female are entirely black except for a yellow-orange throat patch and a thin band of bright blue around the eyes. Immature birds are lighter colored on the breast.

Cormorants are believed to be opportunistic feeders—eating the most abundant and easily available fish resource. No single species of fish dominates their diet, but by 1982, commercial fishermen were beginning to complain that the cormorants were making a significant dent in their whitefish catch—claiming as much as a 30 to 40 percent loss of whitefish due to direct consumption, scarring, or gilling of the fish in the pond nets. Four fishermen who used forty pond nets claimed the loss. Because the birds were protected from destruction, the fishermen attempted to scare them away from their nets by using rubber snakes, wind wheels, brightly colored flags, eagle decoys, and pieces of metal and by covering the nets. Nothing seemed to help.

To try to determine just what fish the cormorants were eating, researchers collected pellets cast by the birds on Gull and Eagle islands. Pellets are compactions of undigested material enveloped in mucous and coughed up by the bird—the same process used by birds of prey. Only adults and subadults expel them.

In many cases the food remains were too well digested to indicate which fish species had been eaten, but researchers looked for otaliths (calcareous concretions found in the inner ear and typical of all vertebrates) not affected by digestion. Studies showed the fish eaten are generally twelve to fifteen centimeters long and the preferred fishing grounds are shallow (five to eighteen meters deep) sandy or shoal areas near the island shorelines. The fish most frequently eaten are the stickleback, slimy sculpin, and burbot—foraging fish rather than commercial. Whitefish and trout were found in 2 percent of the samples studied.

Pond nets serve as convenient perches, and cormorants favor the guy lines and posts. One may see a bird sitting there with wings outstretched as if ready to take flight. This, however, is a behavior of all cormorants. Their feathers lack adequate waterproofing, so after fishing and diving underwater, they try to dry their feathers in the sun and breeze before they fly away.

But who's to say that they don't take advantage of all those trapped fish swimming just below the surface? They have been observed diving into the nets, but rarely seen surfacing with a fish. It is more likely that the fish in the nets are too large for the cormorant to carry, but that in the chase the fish is injured or caught in the net and dies. Young, recently fledged cormorants may contribute heavily in this respect because of their lack of experience in catching fish.

Although they are generally solitary, double-crested cormorants have been observed fishing as a group, in a circle or line formation—herding and concentrating fish for the kill, just as pond nets do.

Various techniques have been tested to keep the cormorants away from the nets. It was discovered that the most effective means was to use a combination of the following; electric shock, nails, cones, and "scarecrows"—dummies attached to the net or sitting in dinghies near the net.

In 1978 cormorants were reported to be nesting on Gull Island. Like the herring gulls, they are colony nesters. Both adults work on the construction of the ground nest, using pebbles, vegetation, and trash gathered from the water's edge or found in diving. Usually three to four eggs are laid, and the incubation period is shared by the parents.

Like the other island nesting birds, cormorants are easily flushed from the nest. They circle overhead, land on the water several hundred meters away, and wait for the disturbance to end. They are wary even after the intruder has left and only return to the island gradually. This means that the adults may be off the nest for twenty to sixty minutes, and if the eggs are still being incubated or the chicks are newly hatched, chances of failure greatly increase. The herring gulls that share the island with the cormorants will quickly seize the opportunity to prey on their exposed nests.

In 1984 some cormorants attempted to ground-nest on Eagle Island, but failed. In 1985 one ground nest was successful; but more significantly, a dozen successful tree nests, made of sticks, were built by cormorants on Eagle Island, and the numbers have increased each year. In the summer of 1987 there were four hundred cormorant nests on Gull Island.

The cormorant will continue to be a source of conflict between the commercial fisherman and the park rules and regulations. Emotions run strong on both sides. It will require compromise and cooperation on the part of the humans involved in this struggle, because the cormorants, who have been around for millions of years, are not likely to change their ways.

BALD EAGLE

Eagles were probably much more common in the Apostle Islands before the addition of DDT in the aquatic food chain. In 1923, the *Bayfield County Press* described an "eagle tree" on Michigan Island—Indians

An eagle's nest can extend 7 to 8 feet across and reach 12 feet in depth. (J. and A. Mahan)

in the area said they had observed the same nest for possibly fifty years and it was active all of that time.

Before the mid-1940s, a pair of bald eagles inhabited every five to ten miles of Great Lakes shoreline. By the 1970s no more than twenty-four breeding pairs remained along that entire area. Those pairs were about equally divided between Lakes Erie and Superior.

Bald eagles are primarily fish eaters, and scavengers to boot—they generally eat fish that are already dead. However, they can capture fish swimming near the surface by grabbing them with strong, sharp talons.

Because they are known fish eaters, they have also been despised by some fishermen, but their impact on commercial fishing is insignificant. However, they are not above thievery. If an unsuspecting osprey carrying a fish flies too near an eagle, it may be chased and forced to drop its catch, which the eagle will then retrieve, sometimes in a midair catch. Eagles also prey on injured waterfowl and an occasional small mammal. The bald eagle really is an opportunist and doesn't seem interested in investing any more energy than necessary in the pursuit of food.

Their diet is in direct competition with the growing population of gulls, and this could very well be a controlling factor in their expansion in the Apostles. Their feeding areas are generally along the shorelines of their

nesting island. They require very large trees (in the Apostles, most often a lonely old white pine that sticks up above the rest) to build their huge nests (seven to eight feet across and twelve feet deep).

After the population dropped from DDT effects in the 1950s, there was not another attempt at nesting in the Apostles until 1980, when a pair nested on Madeline Island. It was not successful. Other nesting pairs began to set up breeding territories on some of the other islands, but none were successful until 1983, when one eagle fledged from Outer Island. During the summer of 1984, nests on Outer, North Twin, and Michigan islands produced two young each, but only four survived to fledge from the nests. In 1986, five eagles fledged from various nests. During the summer of 1987, four eagles fledged from nests on three different islands.

Outer, Devils, Michigan, York, Stockton, Basswood, North Twin, and Rocky Islands have all supported eagle nests in the past few years, although not all of the nests produced young. In the early spring and summer, nests are observed by park employees for activity. If young hatch, they are banded at six weeks. Birds banded in the islands have been found in Florida, at Leech Lake, Minnesota, and in the Mississippi River drainage.

Park Service biologist Merryll Bailey believes that there is still lots of potential eagle habitat in the islands, but that the birds are still fighting the chemical contamination problem. Eggs that have been collected have been found to contain many times more organochlorine pesticides, mercury and PCBs, as well as other chemical contaminants, than eggs from inland Wisconsin, where the eagle population is making a strong comeback. It is believed that the eagles that began to repopulate the Apostle Islands dispersed from the inland lakes of Wisconsin, where decline due to DDT was also felt.

Eagles will sit on a perch, motionless, for hours, just surveying the area around them. One such bird apparently did just that one evening as we ate our dinner anchored in a natural rock cove on Hermit Island. We sat on deck with the setting sun turning the sandstone a golden orange, listening to the wind blowing in the trees and the water lapping against the rock walls. As we pulled the anchor up, a gull came circling around, shrilly calling. That's when first mate Matt Link looked up and saw the reason for the gull's distress call. Sitting calmly on a branch not fifty feet away was a mature bald eagle, its head shining white in the late afternoon sun. Bird and humans watched one another as our boat drifted out of the cove.

That is the closest view we've ever had of an eagle in the Apostles, but we have seen them soaring high overhead as we've cruised by the islands. Their six-to-seven-foot wingspan makes them unmistakable, and when one etches a banking turn and the light flashes off the white head and tail feathers, we know we've seen the embodiment of the spiritual thunderbird.

Bald eagle. (J. and A. Mahan)

DREAM LOTS

The very nature of the Apostle Islands National Lakeshore requires a boat to allow people access to this wilderness area. And boats symbolize more than just travel—they promise adventure, escape, and freedom. A parking lot for boats is usually called a marina, but I call them dream lots. All you have to do is look at the people who wander up and down the docks, with distant looks in their eyes and faint smiles on their lips, to know that they are dreaming of what they would do if they could just find a way to get on one of those boats. It is impossible to suppress the feelings of good fortune when you step aboard a boat, cast off the lines, and leave the dreamers standing on the dock with envious looks in their eyes.

The excitement begins to build long before you reach the marina. On the drive down Highway 13 just before Washburn, Wisconsin, the road dips and turns as it follows the shoreline. First there is a glimpse of the lake, causing the lungs to inhale a little deeper and the heart to pump just a little faster, and then for just a moment, if you're looking at the right place at the right time, there is a break in the trees and you see a forest of masts clustered together. The first tickle of anticipation is felt. As you round the bend and come down the hill that takes you into Bayfield, the whole bay spreads before you, and there's no stopping the smile that spreads across your face.

There is some magnetic force that pulls people down to a pier, where boats rock back and forth. Sound has a lot to do with it—the rhythmic lap of waves against the hulls, the squeaking of rubber fenders pinched between wood and fiberglass, the metallic snapping of wire rigging against aluminum masts, and the discordant cries of the gulls that wheel overhead. It is a romantic place. Couples wander hand in hand, pausing to admire and compare.

There are two breeds of boaters—the sailor and the powerboater. You are either one or the other, and each sees the world very differently. Either you prefer quiet and a leisurely pace or you are thrilled by the throbbing vibration of an engine and the ability to go faster than the wind. In the Apostles, sailboats outnumber power-boats, but both types of boaters feel the same thrill as they gaze at their water "steeds" tied in their "stalls," waiting to be released and set free. It is an analogy I adopted this fall, the boat and the horse—I come with the biases of the sailor and the new owner of a horse.

Whether I walk down the dock to the *Izmir*, the forty-two-foot ketch we sail every summer, or out into the pasture where my horse stands, I feel the same mixture of excitement and apprehension. Both wait patiently as I talk to them in low tones. I know that as soon as I cast off the lines or climb in the saddle there is great power in my hands, but I must remain constantly alert and aware if I am to stay in control. Running with the wind is a sensation of utter joy, living on the edge, doing the impossible, being in control—but just barely. And when I return safely to the slip or stall, I breathe a sigh of relief and exhilaration.

A pleasure boat or a horse is an extravagance. There is no rational justification for spending large amounts of money for their upkeep and safety. And yet they can be very important to our mental health, to our appreciation of living. They bring us moments of magic.

People who own boats become very attached to them. They take great care to pick just the right name. Many of the people who wander in the "dream lot" read and discuss the choice of names. *Sassy Suzy*, *Cat's Paw*, *Victory*, *Izmir*, *Mirage*, *Time Bandit*, *Irish Mist*, *Happy Bottom*—people or place names, descriptions of wind or weather, attitudes and sense of humor all come into play when people choose a name for their boat. Each boat has a personality, special needs and idiosyncrasies, and a name helps to bind the human to the vessel.

There are four major marinas near the Apostles now—three on the mainland and one on Madeline Island. As visitation to the park increases, there will be increased pressure to expand the marinas. It will be necessary to manage the growth of these facilities carefully, for the islands will be able to accommodate and withstand only so much human attention if they are to remain wilderness islands.

(D. Albrecht)

SAILING

It is a world of physics—mechanical advantage, vectors, and forces. It is a land with a foreign language—halyards, vangs, scuppers, and seacocks, where people find themselves suddenly possessing a title on a floating fiefdom. The ruler is the captain or skipper, then there are first, second, third, and fourth mates, all of whom might be collectively called a crew. In races, they acquire titles such as grinders, navigators, helmsmen, and other terms both descriptive and colorful—the color depending on the race results.

Your vessel is an island, like each of the Apostles, an ecology of water, food, and shelter. But it varies from the islands because it moves—it gybes, comes about, lists, planes, runs, reaches, and beats. It is movement that makes your world the strangest of all. The deck is your ground, but it rolls, pitches, and yaws, and it can drop suddenly and then rise just as abruptly.

This is a new world as distinct as a spaceship. Step aboard, but no black-soled shoes allowed. Each step with black soles leaves a mark on board, a perpetual trail and a scar for your sailboat. The boat demands a new lifestyle.

Whether 22-foot or 42-foot, the boat sets the limits of your wandering. It is a private world, but each crew member must respect the others' privacy. It is bedroom, bathroom, kitchen, and dining room, only they are now called berth, head, galley, and saloon.

North, south, east, and west are directions of travel, but they are not good orientation on board, and neither is left or right. Descriptive directions are port and starboard, fore and aft.

Water is everywhere, but it is the water in storage that limits your travels. Fuel capacity for the back-up engine ranks behind the head's holding capacity in determining how long you can live aboard without visiting a port.

Without climbing, you can switch from uphill to downhill. Your stove is gimboled (hinged) so that the pots stay horizontal, but the sailor does not. Paperbacks that are casually set down may become dangerous missiles in stormy seas.

Lying in the sun, feeling the "sea" breeze, enjoying the brace of a fast run are nowhere near the adventure of sitting in the head when the boat switches from 20 degrees port to 20 degrees starboard and the helmsman is laughing because she is imagining the scramble below deck.

There is a rule on board that anyone who is seasick must be aft, but another rule says that in a severe storm all the inexperienced sailors must go below deck, where the motion is the worst. There are times when the rules of safety and the rules of seasickness are not in accordance with one another.

Sailing is an experience, but often it is lack of experience that gives the sailor the most adventure. I can still picture the woman standing with one foot on the dock and one on the deck—pushing off. There was a moment when she wondered whether to step on board or back to the dock. In the time it took her to think of the correct movement, gravity induced her to take a swim.

Then there was the communication problem I had with a crew member. "Pull the dinghy to the foredeck," I ordered. He took the line in hand and made his way to the bow, while I proceeded to back up to the dock. Unfortunately, I forgot to instruct him to hang on to the dinghy line once he got to the foredeck. I knew I should have been more explicit when the dinghy suddenly came in view behind the transom. My realization that it was adrift occurred just ahead of the engine's dying as the loose line wrapped around the prop!

With waves and wind pushing me toward the rocks, I was delighted when my first-mate son hoisted sails and gave me some cloth to catch the wind and sail to safety.

Every sailor has a booklet of stories to tell about engine problems, sails that blew out, lightning, fog, rain, and passengers, especially by the time he or she has logged a few hundred days on the water. Collectively,

In high winds the mainsail is reefed. (J. and A. Mahan)

Overleaf: A quiet anchorage near the sandspit at the southeastern end of Raspberry Island. (J. and A. Mahan)

all these stories can make sailing sound like a masochistic sport, but they are no different than any other sports stories—they are the exceptions, not the rule. Great sports stories are not based on three routine ground balls in the bottom of the first, or the light winds, perfect temperature, and single tack from port to anchor. But it is the untold times, the hundreds of peaceful runs, that are really the story of sailing.

It is quiet movement, relaxation, and peace that prevails on board. Action is condensed into a few moments of raising sail or coming about. For many, sailing may be too quiet, too passive; for others it is the truest form of relaxation.

The speed of a sailboat is measured in knots—single-digit knots. Even when the boat is heeled and the sails are full, the boat is traveling only seven to eight knots. Knots are a measurement of distance that equals nautical miles per hour—one nautical mile is one degree of latitude, or about one and one-fourth statute miles.

Since we can't walk on water, measuring water distance in feet is a waste of time, but the locational grid work of longitude and latitude is significant. North/south, the distance around the globe is fairly uniform, but east/west around the globe varies tremendously from the fat equator to the skinny poles. Nautical miles represent the standard divisions of latitude.

This imaginary grid work is a measure of inner space and gives our ship perspective. With a feeling of speed, but a relatively slow movement compared to other boats and other forms of transportation, we maintain visual contact with our islands for a long time. They grow and fade slowly. Blue haze becomes black/green silhouette, which gives way to individual form, then color, contrast, and detail, at which point the process reverses.

Distant islands blend together without perceptible differences in distance; then we move into the realm of depth perception, the mounds separate by watery corridors, and charts match form and formation.

The sailor has many images of the islands, a series of observations, a continuum of shapes. The islands remain in view for hours and the sailor is constantly watching for safe harbor in case of a future storm. The islands can block wind and wave and funnel them as well.

Like rocky vessels, the islands share the waters of the bay with the sailboats, and both are part of the image of the National Lakeshore.

(K. Crowley)

THE ENERGIES OF SKY AND WATER

The cry "Reef the main!" precedes a scramble on the deck, with sailors clad in bright-yellow foul-weather gear wrestling wind-whipped cloth, and the deck rising and plunging over the waves. The sail is being reefed, shortened and tied to the boom, to reduce the size of the cloth as the wind builds. Spray leaps over the deck, and there is a wild dance within the fiberglass beneath the feet, an exhilaration and determination that masks fear. The foresail reaches out beyond the deck, its foot constantly awash.

The horizon is grey, islands are gone, the water and the sky meld into a distanceless background. The boat careening over the wild swells and madly diving into the next wave, the cloth straining before the force of the storm, is your sanctuary. It is the sailor at the wheel who feels all the forces, senses all the variations in movement and speed. At the wheel the sailor pulls together both earth and sky and feels the immense satisfaction of unifying these two magnificent forces.

★   ★   ★

The sky is dotted with puffy cumulus clouds and the water is scalloped with small waves that march to distant shores. There has been a complex unity of action on the foredeck, and lines and whisker poles suddenly tighten as brightly colored light sailing cloth pops from the chute and a brightly colored spinnaker fills with air. The foredeck rises slightly, the boat moves ahead perceptibly faster, and the sailor catches the waves and surfs forward.

★   ★   ★

It is as though you live on the edge of a mirror. All surfaces above and below seem to be the same. The color of blue permeates your existence, and clouds move slowly above and below you. In the distance ships emerge, upside-down and ill-defined. A single freighter looks like a fleet until it gets near and reassembles in your mind. Fishing boats right themselves suddenly and illusions disappear. It is the sun that bewilders our optic nerves, the heat of midday with no breeze to ruffle the waters, no reference points beside the boat. The curve of the earth hides Canadian lands from our view, but it is not a straight and solid line today. The warmth of bent light rays shimmers and distorts. Mirages that you thought were a product of the desert are just as much a part of the lake. It is the heat. And the sweat beads on your forehead are just as real as they would be on the desert. Your boat sits motionless and you have the option of a quick plunge into Lake Superior's waters. At the end of July a dip into the lake is wonderful.

★   ★   ★

Grey covers a spectrum of today's colors. The dark foreboding grey of a cloud system that seems to roll over the landscape is different from the featureless grey of fog. When the grey seems like it has tentacles and malice and the clouds tumble down the ridge tops there is no place to hide. As you sit anchored in Frog Bay at the end of a secure anchor, this cloud rolls in, pushing wind before it, and the boat shudders and extends the anchor line until it snaps like a whip and the boat halts with a sudden jerking and dipping motion. From side to side the boat lurches and tips, but the wind cannot be escaped; all you can do is peer through the hatches and wait for the calm beyond the storm.

★   ★   ★

Clear skies and a southerly wind mean land-warmed air currents and minimum waves. The wind can generate waves over a distance, but they are barely perceptible where the wind leaves the shore. The distance that the wind moves over open water is called the fetch, and the fetch magnifies the power of the wind in the "zone of action" where erosion sculpts the islands.

A fair sky filled with cottony cumulus clouds. (D. Cox)

Nor'easters are the most dangerous storms, not because they blow hard but because the fetch, the unimpeded distance from Canada to the islands, is greater than the fetch from any other wind. On moderate wind days, the sailor can maximize the cloth on the boat and ride the wind with less concern for the waves.

★ ★ ★

Weather is not only variable, it is dominant in the islands. Even when the sailor seems to have other things to think about, there is an intuition about slight changes in temperature or wind speed and direction. Sailboats lack the speed to outrun the weather systems, so the sailor must anticipate them and prepare for them. No sailor ever fully relaxes who has been on the lake for long. Experience teaches how quickly a doldrum can change to a squall.

Superior is so large it doesn't just receive weather systems; it creates them, it alters them, and at times it strengthens them. The shorelines and the islands all feel the impact of the "lake effect."

The lake "high" can force weather systems to follow the shorelines and miss the water, or the action can be confined to the basin. The results can be impressive. On Devils Island there is no protection for half the wind directions, and the waves surge in with great force to pluck grains from the sandstone and move sediments from rocks to distant beaches and sandspits. Even the vegetation reflects the wind energy. The skyline tapers downward from south to north. The lighthouse end has a forest that resembles the krummholz, the wind-twisted zone at the top of treeline in the mountains. For a few years the winds may be mild and a few adventurous branches will extend beyond the masses, but then a storm arrives to prune the growth and restore the uniformity.

The winds can be so strong that the owner of Steamboat Island journeyed north to visit his private preserve and found that he had been paying taxes on an island that had disappeared during one major storm.

The lake affects the islands and the peninsula in other ways as well. In the winter, when the landscape is locked in ice and snow and the temperatures are dipping well below zero, the open water of the lake remains at a comparatively warm thirty-three degrees and moderates the shore temperature, while providing a source of moisture for winter snowstorms. In a mild winter, less than half of the lake is frozen.

In the spring, the lake keeps the shoreline frost-free, while the mainland fluctuates. The storms at this time create additional hazards, with ice masses moving onto the beaches and scouring the exposed land areas, but for the most part, the economic benefits are greater than the problems. The summer coolness coupled with the extended frost-free period makes this a paradise for fruits, both planted and wild.

The cool damp periods also separate periods of fog — fog so thick that a boat might run aground before it can make visible contact with an island. This is the fog of Maine fishermen, the complete unification of sky and air, with no space between the air moisture and the clouds it spawns. This fog nourishes the succulent plants in the island bogs, puts moisture on the rock-bound lichens, and softens the forest floor.

In autumn, the lake reaches its peak warmth. It takes a long time for the water to absorb the heat of the sun, but it also takes a long time for the water to lose the heat. On land the temperatures rise and fall in a chaos of daily fluctuation, and a fall storm can plunge the landscape into a wintery environment as it moves toward the relatively warm lake. The air above the lake is warmed by the water, and as a result it is light and easily displaced by the cold masses moving over the land. The results are the gales of November, the major storms with oceanlike waves — twenty feet and more in height. This is no time for the sailor; it is a time to stand on shore and watch the solid land succumb to the strength of the fluid motion.

Wind-generated waves break on Point Detour. (M. Link)

Campers on Otter Island watch thunderheads build in the sky behind Oak Island. (K. Crowley)

Sand Island lighthouse. (D. Albrecht)

LIGHTHOUSES AND SHIPWRECKS

The dark brownstone lighthouse was buried in fog, and lighthouse keeper Emmanuel Lueck was tense with his duties. Like all lighthouse keepers, Lueck had an around-the-clock job. For twenty-four hours a day the lighthouse keeper and his assistant and had to maintain a watch. They had to be on there for eight months, April to December, and their duty was to a light and a horn.

They were alone on the islands with their families. They raised gardens and children, played croquet, and polished the lenses. It was a secluded life for the people called "wickies" by mainlanders and boaters.

In the last half of the nineteenth century almost three hundred ships a year were recorded lost in the maelstrom of the Great Lakes. Between 1878 and 1898, six thousand vessels were wrecked. If Lake Superior had fewer than the other lakes, it was only because there was so much less traffic. The lakes had claimed unnumbered lives—immigrants and ships' crews.

The government responded to the situation in 1857 with the Lighthouse Service and a light on Michigan Island. Long Island's lighthouse was built in 1858, and Raspberry's in 1863. Outer Island's light was added in 1874, Sand Island's light was built in 1881, and Chequamegon Point's light in 1895.

Each lighthouse was distinctive in design. The Michigan light looked like a silo on the end of a frame barn, the Outer light was the classical tower of the coast, and the Sand Island structure was made of native sandstone.

The towers' Fresnel lenses were elaborate cut glass hoods made to concentrate a beacon of light through prisms on the top and bottom and magnifying lens on the sides. A kerosene flame provided the light, but if the wick was not trimmed properly the result would be lampblack instead of illumination. Lampblack is a totally opaque soot, and the entire lens had to be cleaned and polished if it appeared. Lighthouse keepers were very careful as a result.

In thick fog, sound was more important than the light, and the keeper was responsible for a fog horn as well. In the early days of lighthouse keeping the men had to blow a horn and ring a bell as a warning. Later the horns were steam-powered with coal boilers. The horns were replaced with airpressure diaphones, beginning at Devils Island in 1928.

All the monotonous days, all the four-hour watches around the clock, all the polishing and the work were meant for days like the one facing Emmanuel Lueck. The fog was too thick to see York Island or the Mainland. It isolated the already secluded lighthouse.

During the long night of gale, the rays of light that could be seen seven miles away on clear nights were absorbed by the clouds and rain. The light did little but illuminate the gloom and the spray of waves crashing on the rocky buttresses of the shore. It was the kind of wild setting that we can only imagine. One lighthouse keeper on Lake Superior had a wave break over his house.

Out in the open water was the *Sevona*, a 373-foot-long steamer, downbound for Sault Sainte Marie. The ship had left port the evening before and pressed against the forces of a full autumn gale. Off Sand Island the situation grew desperate; the ship was in need of shelter, and the islands provided the best opportunity. The islands also presented some of the greatest hazards.

Navigation technology was limited in 1905. Sand Island's light could not be seen from the ship's bridge, and Sand Island had no horn. The boat was in trouble and alone. On the point of land where the lighthouse stood, the keeper had spotted them, and all he could do was watch and wait. He had no motor-powered boat, no radio, no signal that he could turn to. He could only be an observer of tragedy.

On the *Sevona*, the decision was made to seek the shelter of the islands, to head for cover, but their estimated position was in error. They had cleared Sand, but not York, and they turned directly onto the Sand Island shoals, the remnant of an old island that lies eighteen feet below the surface, just below the action of the waves.

The big ship hit and shuddered to a halt. Lueck could do nothing. The lifeboats filled with people on the poop deck, but the main crew was on the foredeck. The large vessel began to come apart, split in half. The lifeboats, filled with wives and family and two crew members, were adrift in ten-to-twenty-foot waves. They tried to reach the foredeck, but the sinking hull disturbed the already turbulent surface with boils and surges as the water entered the hull and displaced the air. The lifeboats were helpless, and the main crew was lost.

The two lifeboats drifted off in the large waves, one to the mainland, where they were found by a homesteader who was looking for a lost cow, and the other to Sand Island, where they found shelter in an abandoned cabin. The lighthouse keeper saw them drift away, and he watched as the rain and the wind intensified and the massive waves broke over the stranded vessel. Then it went down, and Lueck could only wait until rescue vessels came out to hear his story and pick up the bodies, if they washed ashore.

John Irvine on Outer Island was in a similar situation. The steamer *Venezuela* was towing the *Pretoria* through the same September gale when the tow line snapped in the howling nor'easter. The line snapped on both ends and dropped irretrievably into the green water. The boat was loaded with ore and riding dangerously low. This was a freshwater hurricane, and the seas were too much for a floundering vessel.

On shore the lighthouse keeper helplessly watched this midafternoon drama. He saw the *Pretoria* raise a small bow sail to try to gain control of the situation, but it was hopeless. (Rather than eliminate sailing vessels when steam power came in, the shipping companies used them as tow boats, overloaded them, and pulled them across the big lake. Such a boat was beyond maneuverability even if the crew raised all their cloth.)

The sail soon shredded, ghastly streamers for a doomed ship. The anchor was dropped to create a drag. A ship must go either faster or slower than the water's surface to have any control. On a small boat a sea anchor, which looks like a parachute on a line, is used. There were no sea anchors for large ships.

All afternoon Irvine watched the ship rise and fall in the waves. The bow would lift and then disappear, the deck would be awash, the masts would wave frantically, and slowly the boat would drift toward the islands. If they held on, would they run aground where they could gain safety? It was an agonizing wait in the water and on the shore.

As the ship neared Outer Island's northeast point, the anchor suddenly grabbed hold. It was no longer a drag; it now created the worst of all situations—it held the boat in place where the seas could wreak havoc. (When a boat moves, it can ride up and down on the waves. When it is anchored, the line becomes a tether, and the waves batter the stationary craft until it comes apart.) The hatch covers collapsed beneath the stress,

and the seas surged through the vessel—it began to sink.

At 4:05 P.M. John Irvine saw the lifeboat leave the ship with ten men. He raced from the lighthouse to the shore. The lifeboat was taking on water; the combination of men and water left the boat floundering. The odds were against making shore.

Irvine waited on the shoreline. Miraculously the boat was still afloat after a mile. The tension must have been tremendous. Inwardly he must have been cheering, "Come on, you're almost here. Hang on." A thousand feet, nine hundred—they kept coming. Five hundred feet and he could see all ten men. Then four hundred feet away from him a gigantic wave, a rogue in a sea full of rogues, hit them. The impact was stunning, the boat and passengers were thrown into the air and landed near one another in the water.

One by one each of the ten men managed to put a hand on the sunken but floating lifeboat. And then one by one, four men went down and did not surface again.

They got so close that Irvine could see their eyes, even though they were unaware of him. His shouts could not penetrate the wind and waves. Two or three more big waves and they would be on shore. A sailor named Lindloff could not wait. He let go and began to swim, took a few strokes, and sank.

The boat and the remaining five men were catapulted onto the shore in a chaos of foam and spray. The water hit the land and immediately began to rush wildly back to the lake. More water built behind them and tossed them madly about the rocks. The surge outward tugged at their feet while the waves pounded on their backs. They were exhausted, they were on shore, and they were about to be denied life.

But a strong hand from a sixty-year-old lighthouse keeper reached into the white fury and clamped onto the boat. It was a determined grasp that released the tension of over four hours of helpless watching and waiting. He dragged the boat and the survivors to shore. He had made the final difference.

The lighthouse families seldom faced the extremes of this one-day disaster. Most days were mundane, boring. But there were real problems for their own survival, beyond the mental stress. If the ice set too fast, the families had to cross questionable ice paths to the lighthouse service vessels. If personal injury occurred in the family, they had to handle it themselves or wait until the Coast Guard or other boats could come to their rescue.

There are many stories of the families living off wild game until more supplies came. On Raspberry Island the keeper and his son ate all the rabbits they could find and then dug up scraps that had been thrown away in previous meals. These were the times that contrast with the image of the islander as a gardener and croquet player.

Today there is a tranquility at the lighthouses. Motorboats that can travel faster and have more versatility service the volunteers that stay at the lights. The season is shorter, the wicks no longer need trimming,

Lying just offshore is the sunken silhouette of the steamship Fedora. *(J. and A. Mahan)*

Underwater artifacts from the shipwreck Noque Bay. *(S. Heckman)*

Devil's Island lighthouse. (J. and A. Mahan)

the lamps don't require polishing. The lights are automatic now, controlled by radio signals instead of people. Distressed boats radio for help, and electronic gear makes navigation much more exact.

At Outer Island, researchers use the light tower for eagle observations. At Raspberry, Park Service interpreters share the home with visitors.

The volunteers mow the lawn, greet the visitors, and maintain a Park Service presence on the islands. It is a less romantic situation, but the preservation of the lights is important if we are to understand this lake's heritage. The volunteers, like the families of the earlier lighthouse keepers, maintain the energy of life that would be absent in interpretive signs.

The shipwrecks are still there, lying below the clear water. They are protected by the park—cultural artifacts. Their existence adds a dimension to the islands.

The ships went down in action; and like fossils of a much earlier time, they capture something of our history that is emotional and real. They are in the province of the diver now. Silted over, covered by shifting sands, home to spawning fish, dark and cold, they are a place for underwater lights, dry suits, and imagination.

Only recently have the waters of the lake become a divers' domain. For so long the cold temperatures were a serious barrier, but now the divers' equipment extends their capabilities. There is no collecting allowed, but then most collecting is foolish anyway. A rusty bolt looks terrific in context, but on the mantle it merely looks like a refugee from the garbage can. The artifacts of these waters are parts of a large and complex story, and no one has the right to rip out the last page of any book. Find them, leave them, and dream on.

Raspberry Island lighthouse. (J. and A. Mahan)

THE BIG LAKE

There is something special about the imaginary line between the lighthouses on Sand, Devils and Outer Islands. When you cross it, you enter the "big lake." No longer are you in the sheltered waters, where an anchor can isolate you from the storm. No longer do you have warm waters that you can comfortably use for cooling on hot days in July. Out here is where the big boats go, the freighters that carry iron ore to Ohio and grain to Russia. This is the legendary water of Kitchigumi.

Lake Superior lends a special magic to the islands. People who sail the oceans give it special respect because of its coldness and the legendary storms that have sent waves into the second story of Duluth motels.

The sailor, the ecologist, the shipper, the researcher, the commercial fisherman, the cabin owner, the tourist, the park employee all have different views of Superior. In the world, only the Caspian Sea has more area than this lake, and only Lake Baikal has more depth and volume. It has over half the water of all the Great Lakes combined. It has a depth that goes below sea level, and it is shared by three states and two countries.

In the Apostle Islands, we have Chequamegon Bay and the larger Apostle Islands archipelago, but it is a small area in the big pond. There are factors here that no one will face on the thousands of cabin-studded lakes of the Midwest, or in the canoe country. They are the hidden intricacies that excite those of us who study Superior's moods.

Most people are surprised to know that the modern lake is just a young pup among geologic formations, that its entire history is compressed into the last 3500 years. It is a phenomenon of a recent yesterday, which was witnessed by the Indians who lived along the pristine new shores.

Actually the lake is the last stage in a dramatic cast of lakes that followed the departure of the big glacier. The ice sheet swarmed up the ancient river valleys and gouged millions of years of sediment, shaped the islands and the peninsula, and then left in its wake a line of hills that extend in broad, sweeping, connected arches around the entire shoreline.

These tall hills astride the Bayfield Peninsula are part of an interlobate moraine that sweeps south to the old knobs of the Penokean Mountains. The moraine plugged valleys and raised the relief; then the waters that issued forth from the dying ice sheets were trapped and held in deep cold basins that were the first glacial lakes in the series. The different water levels created the Nemadji Stage, Glacial Lake Duluth, Nipissing Great Lakes, and numerous other steps in lake evolution, each stage depositing rich red clay in its depths and sand along its shoreline. Icebergs floated freely in the cold basins; and as they melted, large boulders dropped from the rafts to settle in the clay.

The waters flowed through low spots in the relief, carving river valleys and lowering the lake surface. First there was the Kettle River, then the Brule/Saint Croix, and eventually the Saint Mary River. The surface of the water could never exceed the outlet, and well-defined shorelines resulted.

The story of the lake level was further complicated by the impact of the glacier's weight. It was such a great mass that it actually compressed the rock beneath it, and now that the ice is gone, the earth is rebounding, moving the Saint Mary river from its old position at sea level to its present one 601 feet above the sea.

The river is the lake's drain; the level of the lake is dictated by the level of its outlet. In this complex set of convolutions, the lake has gone from a shoreline 500 feet above the present to one far below the current surface. Superior has been united with the other Great Lakes, and it has been connected directly to the ocean, but before the continental glaciation we have no record of a lake in the area.

This big deep lake has spectacular features besides its huge waves. It is a very cold lake, and the properties of water that cause freshwater lakes to turn over annually have a different result here. Water, like most liquids, gets dense as it cools; the sinking molecules are

Aerial view of Great Lakes freighter emerging from a fog bank. (J. and A. Mahan)

(M. Link)

replaced by warmer ones until the entire basin is uniform, that is, until the temperature reaches 39 degrees Fahrenheit (4°C.), when colder water rises to the surface. Without this phenomenon our winter ice would be on the bottom of the lake, not the top.

In the summer, deep lakes have a thermocline, a place where the water on the upper surface stops mixing with the lower layers—the temperature of the water drops dramatically in inches. Surface waters are riled up by storms, and they mix and absorb oxygen to enrich the waters. Most fish live in this zone, as do all plants. Beneath the thermocline is a dark and mysterious realm of sturgeon and bloodworms.

When the winds push the waters into waves, it is the mixing motor for the oxygen system, and the top zone moves toward the far shore, piling up until the wind relents. The shoreline moves inland or out, sometimes as much as five feet, but there is no tide here. Tide is res-

tricted to the oceans. This phenomenon is called the seiche, and it is even more dramatic than we might realize. The lower levels of the lake tilt beneath the moving surface like the water in a bucket, and when the wind blows and the pressure is released, the layers move back toward stability, just as the water in the carried bucket sloshes back and forth when it is set down to rest.

In the islands this seiche has a special "tidal" effect; it is the way that Chequamegon Bay changes water. This landlocked bay doesn't have much opportunity to exchange waters with the main lake, but the seiche from a north or south wind can rush great quantities of water in and out of this basin. The result is a redistribution of nutrients, which build up in the bay, to the sheltered waters among the islands. It also creates a quick change in temperature.

Temperature in Chequamegon Bay is normally

much warmer than in the lake waters. It is shallow and it has limited contact with the colder basin, but it also is affected by another unusual Superior phenomenon—the spring thermal bar. This bar is an invisible division between the cold lake water and the warm inshore water.

Because of the great depth of the big lake, all those little water molecules, sinking and rising with warm and cold temperatures, have little impact on the overall temperature. Usually we can accurately describe the lake with one word—cold. But the shallow water has a different set of conditions and can warm up well above the temperature of the main lake. In the spring the water sinks as it warms up to 39 degrees Fahrenheit (4°C.), and the sinking extends outward toward the middle of the lake. In the main lake the water is also warming, albeit at a slower rate, and it is also sinking. The result is a vertical column of sinking water that bars the horizontal mix from near shore and midlake. One of the results is a trapping of river deposits, both pollutants and nutrients, in the near-shore zone. This becomes the area of greatest life, and as the summer progresses, this invisible zone of temperature moves further and further "out to sea." The rich spawning waters that satisfy both commercial and sport fishermen benefit from this nutrient trap.

There is a current in the lake as well, a counterclockwise circulation that is another variable in the water mixing. All of this action takes place in the fluid world surrounding the islands. It is a silent system that is as dramatic as anything we can observe, and just knowing that such complexity surrounds us gives us a better measure of the wonders of the earth.

Aerial view of a pond net with a "scareperson" sitting in a dinghy to discourage cormorants from landing and taking fish. (J. and A. Mahan)

Outriggers and skiboards are used to troll for sport fish. (J. and A. Mahan)

FISHING

THE FISHERMEN

The wind whips the light snow up into a mini-tornado, and as it swirls away a figure emerges in the distance. On this expanse of frozen water, it could be 1687 or 1987. The act of catching fish in the dead of winter has not changed dramatically. It continues as it always was, a cold and risky business. The first people to fish around the Apostle Islands wore skins and furs to protect them from the wicked wind. Later fishermen wore woolen clothing. Today, synthetics have been added to the natural fibers, but even with the protection of layers of clothing, hands must be bared to remove fish from the line or nets. Joints, muscle, and skin, exposed year after year to the freezing water and air, finally respond with arthritic pain and paralysis.

Winter is actually a time of relative rest and relaxation for the fishermen of the Apostle Islands. It is a time to repair nets and other gear, a time to visit with each other, reminisce, and play a friendly game of smear. Because as soon as the ice goes out, it will be time to return to the water and the demands of early morning net setting. A fisherman's life is one with little time for vacationing.

Yet when you talk to the old fishermen, they don't speak with regret for the years of hard labor and modest income. They talk about the rewards of independent employment. Like their counterparts on land, the farmers, they are strongly independent people, and their success is balanced between the uncertainties of nature and their own resourcefulness and ambition.

The first fishermen in the Apostles were the Indians who settled there in the sixteenth and seventeenth centuries. Their survival was heavily dependent on fishing. Fish were abundant in the clear, cold waters of the lake—sturgeon, northern pike, trout, whitefish, and herring were eaten fresh or smoked. They used hook and line, spear, weir, and gill nets. The nets were not much different from those used today, only made with the inner bark of bass, willow, or cedar trees and fibers from nettle plants. They were twice the size of a modern tennis net.

In the beginning, they fished only for themselves and their small communities, but then the fur traders arrived and fishing became a means of barter. The early French Canadian explorers were overwhelmed with the size and quantity of fish so easily seen in the clear lake water. Pierre Radisson reported seeing huge sturgeon and pike, seven feet long. Another wrote that in a single night a fisherman could catch twenty large sturgeon, fifty whitefish, or eight hundred herring in one net!

The fur companies at La Pointe, on Madeline Islnd, bought fish from the Indians and then salted the fish, packed them in barrels, and shipped them south or east. In this way the American Fur Company expanded its operations. It was the first to turn a profit from commercial fishing, briefly outstripping its main line of business. But in 1837 there was an economic panic, and a few years later, the fur company was out of the fishing business.

After the Civil War, fishing in the islands began to boom. Scandinavian immigrants were attracted to the area and began to dominate the fishing industry. In 1864 a new innovation, called a pond net (also known as a pound net), improved the industry. It was a net made of webbing, attached to long poles and planted as a submerged well, down to depths of 40 feet. By 1885 there were 185 pond nets off the Apostle Islands! Gill nets were originally made of linen; then cotton was used, it being more elastic. But both required special treatment, and even then their longevity was limited. The more recent use of nylon for nets has increased their life expectancy and made them twice as effective for catching legal-size trout and whitefish.

Manitou Island was the location of one fishing camp. There were many in the islands, but Manitou's history has been researched and documented in recent years, since the Park Service established a special interpretive program there. The current Park Service interpreter, Bill Gordon, is a blend of three ethnic fishing groups: He is a Native American with some French Canadian blood in his background, and as he grew up, he spent his free time learning how to fish from the old Scandinavians in Bayfield.

For almost fifty years, Bill has been involved with fishing on Lake Superior. His hands and face show the lines and roughness that working in the elements bring. He dresses in green work pants, plaid shirt, and suspenders and wears a billed cap that shades his eyes. Bill's arrival on Manitou Island has done more for educating visitors about fishing in the islands than any number of handouts or displays could ever do.

Unfortunately, retirement is rapidly approaching for Bill. He may be looking forward to it, but for those of us who so enjoy his talks in the little cabin about the fisherman's life, his departure will be a sad one.

When boaters arrive on Manitou, Bill is there to greet them. He carries a pipe in one hand and wears his Park Service radio on his hip. He takes out his little notebook and records how many visitors are in the group and then invites everyone up to the grey log cabin.

Once inside, it takes a moment for the eyes to adjust to the dim light. There are only two windows in the cabin—one facing out on the lake, the other facing the woods behind. At one end of the cabin is an old sagging metal-framed bed, and at the other end, a cast-iron woodstove. Hanging on the walls are woolen coats. Bill sits down next to the wooden table in front of the window. On it are arranged some old bottles, a plate, and some fishing lures.

According to local sources, three or four Swedes came out to the island around 1900 to harvest cedar and built the first structure, a cabin built with cedar logs. It wasn't until 1918, or possibly 1920, that permanent occupancy occurred, when a rough old character named Gus Plud (or Plug) took up residence. He had a succession of partners: John Hanson, Harold "Jingling" Johnson, "Black Pete" Lester, and Albert Ditto. The island was owned by the Frenzel Land Co., but the itinerant fisherman were tolerated by squatters. In 1910, the lot consisted of 32.5 acres and taxes were $2.64. Other buildings were added, including a net house, a frame cabin, a small shed covered with metal, a smokehouse, and a dock. To the fishermen, the buildings were known as shacks.

In the late 1930s, the Boutin fishing family operated out of the Manitou camp. They reconstructed and extended the dock. Years of wave action, storms, and winter ice breakup were extremely destructive to docks, and they required regular maintenance.

In 1938, two brothers, Hjalmer and Ted Olson, purchased the camp and 47.2 adjoining acres for $600 from the land company. The Olsons were second-generation fishermen. When Bill Gordon was a young man he came to know Hjalmar, who had developed the nickname "Gov'ner." The Manitou fish camp was a popular spot for fishermen with little or no capital. It didn't attract family groups; for the most part, those who fished and stayed at the site for extended periods of time in the late 1930s and early 1940s were single men.

Bill talks about the hard work involved: "The men would get up around 4 A.M. so they could get out early to raise the nets. They knew that nor'easters generally start to blow around 9 to 10 A.M., so they'd get up early and be out of there." If the weather didn't allow them to get out to the nets, they would work indoors, mending nets or treating the wooden floats. Sometimes in the evening they might play a game of cards. But generally it was early to bed, early to rise.

There is always risk and danger involved when the fisherman goes out in his boat. Theirs were open wooden boats twenty to twenty-four feet long and five to six feet across, powered by small gas engines. According to Bill, it takes time and practice to learn the ropes. "Fishermen are familiar with the landmarks on these islands. I never go out too far when I'm alone. I might go as far as Bear. I'm a fair-weather fisherman now. I don't go out in my little boat except in calm water. You never know what you're facing. The wind can come right around 180 degrees in a few minutes."

Bill knows that some fishermen drink too much and go out in their boats. He knows how unwise this is, because "You really got to be ready for the changes that can come up." He tells a story about one fisherman who went into Bayfield for a little relaxation, left in his boat, and was never seen again. That was the destiny of fishermen Hanson and Ditto in November 1935. They had been in Bayfield, and on their return to Manitou, they stopped at Otto Kung's Harbor Lodge, just north of Red Cliff, to have their boat's engine repaired. They set out again in their twenty-foot open boat, but never reached Manitou. The *Bayfield County Press* at that time wrote that it was "believed likely that the two men were carried out into Lake Superior."

After talking and answering questions inside the cabin, Bill tkes his visitors outside to show them the smokehouse, nets, and other sheds. At the smokehouse, he explains the process used to get the best product. "I use maple to get the best smoked flavor and I leave the scales on the fish. It makes them really stand out nice. I think the old fishermen did that. You gotta have a good product as well as a good-looking product."

Nets are wound around the wooden reels, and Bill likes to demonstrate to his visitors how to sew a net and then give them a chance to try it. He says, "They get more of a feel for it, than just listening to me talk." Bill tells how in the old days a fisherman kept track of his helpers: "The reel would normally squeak when it went around, so if the fisherman was sitting in the cabin, smoking his pipe, he would listen for that sound—that way he'd know the help was still working."

The nets on the reels are just used for demonstration. Over by his living quarters, Bill has another net under construction. This is one he's making in his spare time for his own use. Even though he says "You can't make a gill net today and get your money out of it, if you take into account your hours," he's always made his own. He figured he would make twelve nets during the summer months, worth about $2,000.

(J. and A. Mahan)

People always ask Bill whether he doesn't get lonely out at the island all by himself, but he reminds them, "There are people out here all the time." Besides, "There is always something to do. I never have a day off. If the weather's calm and I'm not working on nets, I might take my little boat and go over to my cabin on Raspberry Bay."

Retirement is something Bill doesn't plan on doing entirely. He says, "I'll be doing some fishing and I'm going to get one of those little power winches for my nets." Bill summarizes his choice of career in this way, "It takes a special type of person to be a fisherman. Gotta take the disappointment with the good. It all averages out to a good living."

THE FISH

Mike and I were exploring the Hokanson Brothers Fishery at Little Sand Bay, and as we walked out on the dock, we noticed activity on the *Donna Belle.* She is a typical Lake Superior fishing boat—squat and white, with a flat roof and a few small round portholes in the raised cockpit. We walked out beside it, and in the dark and cluttered interior we could see the bottom half of two figures moving around in their bright yellow rain pants. On a wooden table and in boxes of ice were silvery stacks of fish. The men were methodically slicing, cleaning, and rinsing the fish. We walked toward the back of the boat, leaned down, and peered in. Eventu-

ally one of the men noticed us and stuck his head out and said hello.

The Park Service allows fisherman John Erickson to tie up at the Hokanson dock after collecting his day's catch, and often he will take the time to talk to visitors like us, who wander down with questions about the boat, the fish, or the work in general. It makes the place feel a little less like a museum, and it also gives people a chance to see fresh samples of the fish that soon will be filleted and served in the area's restaurants.

Whitefish, lake trout, and herring have been the mainstays of the fishing industry in the Apostles region. Their abundance has fluctuated; and at various times, each species was the most popular and valuable catch.

Lake trout have accumulated many other common names, including landlocked salmon, silver trout, paperfin, rock-of-ages trout, siskiwit, and mooneye. They are greyish, with pale spots on the darker background and deeply forked tails. They make up about three quarters of the trout caught in Lake Superior. Preferring temperatures around 50 degrees, they move to deeper water as the summer season progresses. They are predators, and their favored food is other fish, such as ciscoes and smelt. Insects rank second in their food preferences. Trout rank very high on the food list for fish lovers. They have a firm, slightly pink flesh with a delicate flavor, reminiscent of their relative, the salmon.

Lake trout have a strong homing instinct and will return to spawning sites. They used to spawn up streams, but pollution forced them to find other suitable spawning areas. These days, during the fall, eggs are broadcast and fertilized over broken, rocky reefs, such as the shoals off Gull and Michigan Islands. After five months of incubation, the little trout hatch and feed on the zooplankton. It will be six to seven years before they are fully mature. Fewer than one in twenty stocked trout survive the hazards of being a fingerling, and it's even worse for those hatched in the lake — only one in one thousand will live to maturity. The cold water can mean a long life, if the trout can avoid the efficient commercial fishing methods. A lucky old trout may grow to weigh as much as 40 pounds, although 4 to 22 pounds is more common.

In the early 1900s, lake trout were the most valuable commercial fish in the Great Lakes, and remained so for almost fifty years. The annual harvest was 350,000 pounds, but this kind of continual pressure and the introduction of sea lampreys during the 1950s and 1960s decimated their population. Today, the sea lamprey has been controlled, and stocking programs are encouraging the trout to repopulate the lake — a reason for rejoicing for the sport fisherman, the gourmand, and the naturalist.

Lake whitefish livers are a delicacy among Bayfield and Apostle Island lovers of fine food. They have a rich but nonfishy flavor. Some prefer them deep-fat-fried, while others find them most delicious sauteed in butter and served on a bed of wild rice. The rest of the fish has also been prized for the quality of the meat. A scientist in 1836 was quoted as saying "We can say from personal experience that a diet of whitefish alone, with no other food, can be eaten for days without losing its appeal."

Whitefish are the color of newly polished silver. They once reached weights of 20 pounds or more, but because of periodic overfishing and the destructive lamprey, their size and abundance has dramatically decreased. Now a whitefish weighs between 1.5 and 8 pounds and reaches 17 to 27 inches in length. They are not a popular sport fish in Lake Superior, but are a heavy commercial target. These fish travel in the deep cold water during the summer months, occasionally running into the deep-set gill nets, providing the fishermen with their livelihood. One study of tagged whitefish that were recaptured showed that they migrated less than five miles during a season and that the whitefish in the Apostle Islands region are one of a number of distinct stocks in Lake Superior. There is no limit on the number of whitefish caught, just minimum size. They are also protected during fall spawning, which also occurs on reefs and shoals.

"Pickled" is usually the word that comes to my mind when herring is mentioned. It is a traditional Scandinavian food and one that non-Scandinavians like myself have come to consider a special treat, especially around the holiday season. **Lake herring** are small relatives of the larger lake whitefish. They average 12 inches and weigh between 6 and 24 ounces.

Traveling in large schools, they have been the source of the greatest commercial catch of any Great Lakes fish in the last one hundred years. They are low on the food chain in the lake ecology, feeding on plankton, insects, and eggs, and becoming the food for larger fish as well as people. They were an important staple in the diet of the early settlers in the Apostles region, often being smoked or salted down for longer storage. Lake herring were an important source of income for the fishermen on Manitou Island. The fish would be processed and packed in 115-pound-capacity kegs in a shed at the end of the dock and then sent to Bayfield and points beyond.

In late fall, usually a week or two after the whitefish have spawned, the herring swarm into the shallow water and lay their eggs. These fish have suffered the same fate as the other species, falling victim to pollution and overfishing, as well as being outcompeted by the accidentally introduced smelt. The once large schools of herring have dwindled, and state stocking efforts have been initiated to try and revitalize their population.

A commercial fishing boat in the harbor at Cornucopia, Wisconsin. (K. Crowley)

(J. Steinke)

SETTLEMENT

The islands are healing themselves, slowly burying the little human treasures. With each passing year, the plants grow a little thicker in the clearings and the old people's memories fade, pushing the human history of these islands further into the mists. Back in the forest, a flaming orange daylily blooms, a lilac bush releases its scent as if from an antique bottle partially buried in the leafy soil. A red squirrel tears apart a pine cone while perched on an overturned grey enamel coffeepot. Wild strawberries vine around the handle of a black iron kettle. All bits and pieces left by the people who came to the Apostles with hopes of making a fortune—or maybe just a modest living.

They were an energetic lot—loggers came in and stripped the land of its old forest, quarrymen cut into the rock and hauled away pieces of the islands, hopeful farmers cleared away rock and tree and sought to make the land produce vegetables and fruit, and finally entrepeneurs, trying to entice fishermen and tourists, built cabins and restaurants near the sandy beaches.

Some of the stories are well documented, but most are based on the subjective and imaginative memories of the people who knew a relative or a friend who lived in those earlier days. Other than Madeline, Sand was the only island to support a fully functioning community. It was established for the people who came to farm and fish. The first, Francis W. Shaw, arrived in the 1860s. He received his land as a bonus for serving in the Civil War. The *Bayfield County Press* in 1888 called him Emperor of Sand Island.

In 1902 "Governor" Samuel Fifield, a strong local proponent of the islands, bought land on the southeast corner of the island and established a summer resort. Known as Camp Stella, it began with a frame house and a tent colony, but expanded into a series of frame cottages. They were unique structures, many made from the hatch covers of the steamer *Savona*, which sank just offshore.

In 1910 Shaw's son-in-law, Burt Hill, moved to Sand Island to join his father-in-law in the fishing business. He was an ambitious man who tried farming, became postmaster for the five years that the post office existed, and organized the Sand Island Telephone Company and the retail store. The last two ventures ended in failure—the phone company because the cable was cut by passing boat traffic, and the store for lack of enthusiasm by the other townspeople, who could just as easily get their groceries from the boat that came every day to pick up their fish.

The schoolhouse was built in 1910. The first class had thirteen students. The schoolhouse also served as the gathering place for many community picnics. A community smokehouse and icehouse completed the town buildings.

Another resort area developed in 1912, when six families founded the West Bay Club on the west side of the island. This establishment included cabins and a clubhouse.

Scattered throughout the islands were fishing cabins, and on a few islands log farmhouses and barns, but the most famous "cabin" was built on Hermit Island. Known locally as the bark cottage, it was built in the mid 1890s by the owner of the sandstone quarry, a Mr. Prentice. He named it Cedar Bark Lodge. Its walls were entirely covered with the bark of white cedar, also known as Indian shingles. An old photo shows a three-story structure with a turret in front and a large water tank in back. Legend says that Prentice built it for his bride, but she didn't appreciate it as he did and refused to live there. It stood until the 1930s, when it was finally torn down.

An effort was made to sell building lots on Hermit Island in 1910, but that venture proved unsuccessful, too.

Rocky and South Twin islands face one another across a narrow, shallow channel of water. It was one of the most popular sport fishing areas, for trolling. Rocky Island was owned by Henry Rice, a Wisconsin senator and one of the founders of Bayfield. He established a resort on the eastern shore, with cottages and

Village of La Pointe on Madeline Island. (J. and A. Mahan)

Many historic buildings still exist in La Pointe on Madeline Island (D. Albrecht)

a restaurant for the summer visitors.

Competing for business on the western shore of South Twin Island was another small resort and restaurant, built shortly after World War II by a couple from Oregon. They sold out to their partner in the early 1950s. He brought a bulldozer and a car to the island and then put an airplane runway on the island. Hikers still use the grassy strip, to walk from the campground to the end of the island.

On Basswood Island, known in the late 1800s as Bass Island, there were several farming homesteads. One belonged to Richard McCloud and his brother, Joseph, who was a county judge. It may be that the judge also used his property as a tourist location, because in 1880 he was identified in a local publication as the proprietor of the Bass Island Hotel.

Oak Island had some fishing cabins and logging camps, but it was looked at by some as a potential site for "hospitals or water care establishments" because "Splendid springs burst their crystal waters from its sides, and flow in silvery springs into the lake." Imaginative plans that never materialized.

The Apostle Islands were owned by private interests and could have become the secluded sanctuaries of the rich and famous, but through the efforts of far-sighted individuals and groups, they were incorporated into the National Park system in 1970. The effort to bring them into the public domain was a long, emotional, and difficult struggle. In 1930, when the drive first began, the islands showed the scars of logging and fires and were not considered attractive enough for a National Park. It was also believed that it would take fifty to one hundred years for them to regain their forest cover.

In the early 1960s enthusiasm once again returned, and in 1965 Senator Gaylord Nelson of Wisconsin introduced the first bill to establish the Apostle Islands National Lakeshore. Between 1965 and 1970 many public hearings were held to discuss the proposed plan. Finally, in September 1970, President Nixon signed the bill that set aside twenty of the twenty-two Apostle islands for present and future generations to treasure and enjoy.

★ ★ ★

This old log cabin on Manitou Island has been restored by the Park Service and is part of their interpretive program for park visitors. (K. Crowley)

Fishing boats work as long as there is open water. (K. Crowley)

WINTER

It's morning and the sky seems thick with clouds. Light flakes drift down to break the greyness and settle on the lawns. They are big flakes, falling a very short distance. The accumulate in soft foamlike thickness, their large crystal points rising from the whiteness like a fringe.

The sky begins to break up about midmorning. The thick cloudmass fragments into low cumulus clouds, and a brilliant blueness spreads out from the horizon. Sunshine reveals the morning mirage, the relatively thin cloud cover that appeared so thick and heavy only because we were within it. The afternoon will be brilliant, and the sunshine will sparkle on the fresh winter coat.

In the open water a cold steam rises from the stillness of the lake. This is water vapor, barely removed from its liquid state. Winds whip it into wispy tails on the surface, and the lake looks like a giant cauldron during the day. But at night the vapor condenses into thick fog that grows into stratus clouds, thick moist clouds that are not suspended above the ground. In the morning the sunshine stirs the air molecules, warms and moves the air. Light winds push from the northern shores and displace the lake air. It is cold air, heavy from Arctic influence, that moves the warmer Lake Superior air with relative ease. The fog moves onto land and cools on the south shore. The quick freeze of vapor into crystals gives the moisture substance, and the closely packed crystals adhere to one another until they tumble from the cloud by sheer weight.

Once free of the cloud, the flat disk of snow drifts on air eddies, floating and gently settling in a new morning dusting. This is lake-effect snow.

Of course, there are times when the snows are more than flakes, when the storms seem to suck up all the moisture of the lake and dump piles of snow that are measured in feet. These are the real winter storms, the blizzards, the bonanza of the cold months.

At Christmas, the Rittenhouse Inn in Bayfield is festooned with garlands of pine and white lights that contrast with its red siding. Up the block, Mary Rice's home is subtly decorated in white lights. It is the only thing subtle about this beautiful structure, and in the corner windows decorated trees shine, one above the other, on each floor of the mansion. There are white lights on the Christmas shop too, and the entire town seems quietly festive.

Sailboats sit in their cradles, ice flows shift along the rocks at Houghton Point, and the ferry motors back and forth to Madeline. Soon the bay will freeze and a wind sled will replace the boats for a short period when ice and water are intermingled and unsafe. Then the bay will become solid, and the county will declare it a road, perhaps the only county road in the country with a three-month life in the best winters. Discarded Christmas trees are placed along the new road, an instant holiday forest, and the county road crews include this route in their plowing and maintenance schedule. It is the only road in Wisconsin that never has a pothole.

The streets of Bayfield are quiet, and La Pointe has only its native population of hardy winterers. There are only a few stores open in the winter, and the inns and lodges have vacancies. The Self-Propelled shop rents cross-country skis, unless a winter diver decides to investigate the warmer water environment.

In Cornucopia, the Russian Orthodox church looks like it is in a Moscow winter. The state's northernmost post office looks like it is in polar regions, and icicles replace gulls on the harbor barn.

In mid-peninsula, Valhalla lives up to its name for the Nordic skiers on their skinny skis. This is the Forest Service ski center, and there are loops through forests of northern hardwoods, oak, and pines. The trails skirt old beachlines and drop down wave-cut benches of ancient lake levels. Weasel, deer, grouse, and hare leave tracks in the snow, and ravens do aerial ballets, accompanied by their own coarse barks.

In Little Sand Bay, the Hokenson Brothers Fisheries is blanketed in whiteness, and the docks are curtained with ice. There is a silence in the woods, but the sounds are rich in the peopleless bay. Ice waves have frozen in a winterlong trance beside the rigid sands, but beyond them the water responds to the winds and energies of the lake. The ice mantle breaks with the insurgent energies of the lake. The ice fractures in the rolling surf, pounds against itself, rolls, grates, and redefines itself and then refreezes into a parquet of round disks.

Beyond the dock the ice has gone from round disks to ice chimes, small ice fragments that ring against one another as the waves roll in. The dock has hollow ice domes that accept the waves and the wind in alternating flows that resonate like the deep breathing of a very placid sleeper.

Silent sports seem most appropriate in this area. The resorts have not discovered how to attract the skier like other places have, but soon the message will be out and the trails of Valhalla and Mount Ashwabay will not be enough.

Skiers will discover the silent sweep of beach in Big Bay State Park and the stately conifer forest, and they will demand trails that allow them the protection of the woods and the expanse of open lake.

We visited this beach just before New Year's. It was empty; only the wind in the pines gave sound to the scene. The moist areas of sand were solid, while in places the surface crispness gave way to soft dry sand below. The tan grass stalks made white snow patches look tufted, and the sprawling, spreading junipers were frosted. On the beach was a giant waterbug, frozen in place. Two inches long, large pinchers imbedded in ice, this watery predator was caught up in the winter landscape, an imprisoned participant in the quiet season, while the six of us who explored the shore found joy in the contrasts of the season that so few people know in the islands.

An icy sea cave near Little Sand Bay. (D. Albrecht)

PERSPECTIVES

The Apostle Islands are a part of the heritage of Lake Superior. They are not distinct from one another; they are instead a discrete unit within a complex geographical system that is defined by the drainage basin of the most expansive freshwater lake in the world. They have suffered and survived quarrying, logging, tourism, agriculture, fishing, storms, fluctuating lake levels, acid rains and snows, and the elimination of native species, along with the introduction of alien weeds and animal pests.

Like the lake itself, these islands represent the resiliency of nature. Given a chance, nature can maintain itself, adapt, adjust, and be beautiful, inspirational, and viable. What we don't know yet is *how* resilient nature is; we do not know when the bending will become a break. In the Apostles the designation of National Lakeshore assured the survival of the rare beach plants and saved the nesting colonies from the destruction of development. Long Island was added to protect the piping plover, but we will not know for many years whether this action came in time or too late.

While the park protects the area from one type of development, it also engages in its own development, and like all parks it has the job of encouraging visitation. It must provide campsites, but in doing so, it must sacrifice some natural areas. If not, people will find campsites that are unsuited to human uses. Some of these already exist — they are set back out of the natural protection of the wind and the sun and become areas of human sacrifice to the myriad swarms of biting flies.

Tourists who want to visit the islands need access, so excursion boats become larger, and their wakes wash up on sensitive shorelines with increased erosional power. New accesses increase powerboat use and make remote sandspits more popular and more impacted. Structures on the islands to accommodate the visitor are actually changing the sights the visitor will see. The old fishing shacks are gone from Stockton, and the new visitors will never know the old island. They will instead visit a recreational marina that is maintained by the Park Service.

It is all compromise, and the Park Service can be caught in the middle, just as they were when a Washington official had the idea that they could sell off Sand Island after the park was already established. These islands and this park need the vigilance of people who care, but our concern must reach beyond the Apostle Islands to the lake itself. The Apostles, Isle Royale, and the Flint Islands of Canada are just pieces of the biological pie. Lake Superior is the common thread, and whatever happens to the lake will affect all the preserves, and ultimately all of our lives.

In a paper with a lengthy title, "Vision Superior: Rationale and Statement of Intent of the International Coalition for the World's Last Great Lake," Bruce Littlejohn drafted the position for a 1987 Lake Superior Ecosystem Workshop. The following paragraphs give a sense of purpose for a united concern about Lake Superior.

"Among the major environments which have geographical and ecological integrity in the industrialized world, that of Lake Superior and its drainage basin is unexampled. Put simply, there is no other freshwater body that can compare with it in magnitude, natural quality, and sheer beauty.

"Given the Lake's proximity to one of the most heavily populated and heavily industrialized regions of the world, and given the high degree of environmental degradation which has become commonplace in such regions, it is amazing that Lake Superior retains an impressive degree of purity and wildness. For the moment it survives in the heartland of North America as a symbol of hope for a world that no longer makes ecological sense — a world marked by excessive and wasteful consumption of resources, population outbreak, rapid and often irrevocable depletion of natural habitats, unprecedented rates of extinction and the reckless release of toxic pollutants. As such, its worth, in both real and symbolic terms, is inestimable.

"Lake Superior is, then, both ark and icon. As ark, it is a repository of living things which are threatened by the rising flood of toxins and the exploitive tidal wave of human activities based on short-term economic advantage. As icon, it survives as a symbol of hope to all those who love life in its totality, who strive to preserve nature's integrity and diversity, and who look to a better and saner future in which human actions are predicated on survival and the long-term health of our environment."

If this seems like an overstatement, it is only because Lake Superior's great size and depth, and the limited population living right on the lake, have masked the problems. We can remember the controversies over asbestos in the tailings of Reserve Mining, the introduction of alewives and lampreys into the ecosystem, the massive erosion from the red clay shorelines during the high water years of 1985 and 1986, and the threats of acid rain and PCB contaminants, but each battle seems separate and distant. So far Superior's size has saved it, and we still have the largest and purest basin of fresh water in the world.

The Apostles are one important piece in the crown of Lake Superior, and we must take care of them, while safeguarding the entire region.

ABOUT THE AUTHORS

Mike Link has an enthusiasm for adventures—adventures as diverse as paddling a wild river, sailing the open seas, observing a wild bird, keying out a new flower, or reading a good book. Each experience is a challenge, and each new assignment is an opportunity. Mike has two children, Matt and Julie, who have shared outdoor experiences with their father.

As director of Northwoods Audubon Center, Mike also is an instructor in outdoor education for Northland College and the University of Minnesota at Duluth. His published works include *Journeys To Door County*, *The Black Hills/Badlands*, *Outdoor Education*, and *Grazing*, and numerous magazine and newspaper articles.

Kate Crowley's skills as a naturalist and writer were developed during her nine years at the Minnesota Zoo, where she supervised the monorail interpretive program and wrote articles for zoo publications. Her knowledge of wildlife and wilderness grew with participation in volunteer bird censusing for the Minnesota River Valley Wildlife Refuge and exploration of wild lands in the U.S. and abroad. She has served for five years on the board of the Minnesota Naturalist Association.

Kate is the proud mother of Alyssa and Jonathon. Her interests include almost any outdoor activity, especially sailing and bird-watching and more recently, exploring her new home in Willow River, Minnesota, with Mike.

Mike and Kate were married aboard the ketch *Izmir* and sailed Lake Superior on their honeymoon. They are coauthors of a new series for Voyageur Press covering wildlife and wild lands.

(K. Crowley)   672-2
                5-18
                C
                S

96